MAKING SMART CLOTHES

MODERN
METHODS
IN
CUTTING
FITTING
AND
FINISHING

The evolution of a frock reveals the individuality, economy and simplicity of MAKING SMART CLOTHES

CONTENTS

I. **FOREWORD**

II. **MAKING SMART CLOTHES**

    Individuality—Economy......... 2

    Personality in Patterns.......... 4

    Flattery in Fabrics 7

    Character in Colors 9

    Safe Shopping Guides......... 14

    Pattern Adjustment 16

    Modern Methods of Cutting 24

    The Science of Basting 35

    Modern Methods of Fitting 39

    Finesse in Finishing............ 50

    Modernizing Your Wardrobe.... 103

    Professional Pressing........... 109

III. **MAKING SMART CLOTHES KEEP THEIR FRESHNESS**........ 114

IV. **INDEX** 123

FOREWORD ....

To that great army of wise women who appreciate the supreme importance of being well dressed ... who know that the only economical way to attain smart, individual and perfectly fitting clothes in good taste is to make their own ... Butterick dedicates this ultra modern book on modern dressmaking designed to make home sewing as easy and pleasurable as it is economical.

Here in the step-by-step evolution of a smart frock Butterick has crystallized the formula for all successful dressmaking ... a formula which resolves itself into these three factors ... the choice of a superlatively smart style in a good pattern ... smart fabric in a becoming tone and texture, correctly cut ... and perfect workmanship.

Experts have reduced each of these three factors to their simplest terms. Fascinating chapters on line, color, and texture reveal the importance of careful selection of pattern and fabric, teach you to know yourself, and unlock new doors to beauty and charm. Step-by-step, experienced dressmakers lay down the a, b, c, of cutting, fitting and finishing, explaining briefly and directly, demonstrating with pictures, the essentials of perfect workmanship. They have performed for you all the costly time-consuming experimental work that might have made your homesewing a hazardous venture, and every crumb of knowledge gleaned from constant laboratory work has gone into their explanations of dressmaking methods—modern methods that will impart to your clothes that distinctive "custom-made" air.

Dressmaking books, as you well know, are not made for the ages but for the day of current fashion. When fashions change methods of dressmaking change with them and you must have the new methods. For the busy business woman ... for the homemaker of many interests, "Making Smart Clothes" is the logical guide to successful dressmaking because it is completely in step with the new fashions. Its authoritative pages will give you confidence in your own creative ability.

GRACE C. DIMELOW

MAKING SMART CLOTHES
INDIVIDUALITY . ECONOMY

When fashion suddenly goes topsy-turvy

Whenever the fashion world suddenly startles us out of our complacency by turning everything topsy-turvy and ordaining such things as waist-lines which have long been hidden and forgotten, rippling folds to cover kneecaps that have long flamed unabashed, and other drastic innovations, there is a helter-skelter dash to assemble an entirely new wardrobe. It is discovered that it is impossible to lengthen hems that are finished by binding; that it is perfectly possible to put a belt high on last year's dress, but you never know what strange bulges are going to appear below it. Things have to be new, brand new. This is always perfectly charming for those who can rush headlong into Mme. Chanel's or the atelier of a smart New York dressmaking house and order lavishly, but, for those of us who can't throw out last season's mink coat without a slight qualm it is a bitter blow. Fashion ought really to be more considerate and do things a bit gradually.

Such revolutionary changes, keeping pace with modern ideas, occur so frequently that shopping is not the simple matter it once was. Once you could buy a little two-piece dress you fancied, take in the hips, lengthen the sleeves, shorten the skirt—all straight up and down alteration that a child could do—and march out in triumph with a dress that, to all outward appearances might have been made for you. But nowadays these frocks with the little crisscross bias pieces moulding the waistline or intricate pointed godets contriving with subtlety to fit an intriguing hip-line are not so easy to alter.

Couturiers listen to reason

American women frequently forget that all women with a great reputation for chic, both here and abroad, have a great deal to say about the making of their own clothes. They may go to M. Lelong, pick out a good model, and have him make it, amidst French purrings and outcries, but they select their own material; they demand that the neck be deeper or the skirt fuller; they make every detail conform to their individual figures. In the end, the dress is their own dress; it is not a carbon copy. Other women go to little French copyists, whom they watch like hawks through several fittings. But all really smart women, we repeat, have the general lines and colors and fabrics and adaptations of a model under their own personal control. And that is why they are photographed at the races at Longchamps or Belmont, and why fashions change if they appear in new ones.

Not all of us can go to a French couturier, or even to a French copyist to assemble our wardrobes for the season. American custommade places are fearfully expensive, and those exquisite little dressmakers have been snapped up so thoroughly by eager shops that anybody finding one should lock her up in the safe nights. These days the only way to stamp one's individuality on a wardrobe is to make one's own. **You don't have to be an expert**

Every intelligent woman who knows how to pick out good fabrics and has the sense to follow good directions can make a better dress for fifteen dollars than she can buy for thirty-nine fifty. She can make an infinitely better dress, it goes without saying, for fifteen dollars than the little bargain she picked up for sixteen-fifty that, somehow or other, looks so frail and weak after that first exhausting trip to the cleaners.

If it were very, very difficult to make smart clothes at home we wouldn't be beating the war drums of individuality this way. We wouldn't betray our fellow womenfolk into the hands of a nervous collapse made horrible by the visions of pink and green sewing machines crawling up the wall. But you don't have to be an expert to make a chic dress. You may not have the God-given genius that gives M. Patou the authority to revolutionize the fashion world; but then you may not have the wisp of inspiration that makes a great French chef. But, if you use your common sense and a good cook book, you can learn to turn out a deliciously edible meal in no time at all; with the same common sense and a good pattern—and you may have three guesses as to which patterns we think are the best— you can create a dress that a rich relative would envy. **Common sense and a really good pattern**

Few of us who do not declare independence of "ready-mades," can find our favorite color, line, and fabric in the same dress. Successful home dressmakers remember the following axioms: (1) never economize on fabric; good material may be worn to pieces and never look shoddy; (2) always buy exactly the amount of fabric designated on your directions; skimping always shows; (3) always hold the paper pattern against you to be sure of length and width and general fitness before you slash into your treasured length of silk; (4) don't copy department store Fords; only unoriginal people wear uniforms; (5) pick out lines that are becoming to your figure and, if you are uncertain how to do this, read further, for we go into constructive detail on these fine points. **Five rules for smart dressmaking**

Above all, keep your sense of adventure about clothes.

MAKING SMART CLOTHES
PERSONALITY IN PATTERNS

Frocks should be gay, charming and frivolous and delightful, not grim, haggling, budget-bound necessities. Do you want to be just covered, or do you want to be the centre of attraction wherever you go? The choice is in your own hands, and in your own artistry.

You'll need a truthful mirror and a good light

In fashioning a dress for yourself (and must I keep telling you and *telling* you that this is the only economical and original way to true smartness?) it is not possible to try on several dresses before deciding which will be the most becoming. Most of us realize vaguely that certain lines are more flattering to us than others, without ever stopping to think of the mathematical and structural reasons for this. The first step for every woman eager for the adventure of creating clothes, then, is to secure a full length mirror, a brutal light, a kind but catty friend if possible, and a detached attitude of mind in studying her figure.

Once you have faced the reality of your construction by this method, you will be equipped to select a pattern that makes the most of your good points and conceals the bad ones. And you won't insist on choosing a charming little frock that looks ravishing on the petite Mrs. Goodenough if you chance to be five feet ten, with a net tonnage of two hundred pounds.

Consider the matter of necklines

For instance, necks. Women with short necks should not make them appear shorter by Garbo bobs or hats with long brims in back. They should never wear picture hats that, from a rear view, make the head one with the shoulders and eliminate the neck altogether. They should never cut the line of the throat with mammoth choker necklaces. For them, are the deep V necklines that lengthen the neck; the collarless, or nearly collarless mode. Only long necked women should wear towering fur collars, lingerie touches that simulate a Pierrot ruff, and Egyptian jewellery at the collarbone.

Skirt-lengths may be kind but often cruel

Circular skirts that flare smartly below the hips make both hips and legs seem smaller. The piano-legged and the bowlegged woman alike should be terribly careful never to put them in silhouette by means of dresses cut short in front and terribly long in back. Peek-a-boo, uneven hemlines are the greatest help to such as these, when they are permissible. If the legs above the knee are large, never wrap a dress tightly across this point. You would think that everyone would know this, but there seem to be thousands of women who never look in a mirror except to see whether or not their noses are shiny.

If your hands are big, avoid tight cuffs. If your arms are thin, and you still insist on being fashionably sleeveless for evening, remember that floating pieces hanging from the shoulder or underneath the arm have a coy way of wafting about and partly enveloping the arm in an attractively seductive manner.

Sleeves make black magic

Large bosomed women should avoid those loose, casual bows over the chest in the Vionnet manner; boyish women who crave feminity should greet them with shrieks of joy.

Shoulders are another point of study. A woman with broad shoulders is lucky, for her hips will usually seem small by comparison. If the shoulders are a bit too broad, she must be careful to set in her sleeves high on the shoulder; she may greet with cheers, sleeves in the raglan manner; she should avoid, like Welsh rarebit at four in the morning, those little cap sleeves that Chanel delights in, short flaring capes, or the mode of putting decoration on the upper arm. All those frills that build out the shoulder are for the woman with narrow shoulders who wants to bring her hips back into proportion.

We are going to harp a great deal on the narrow shouldered, broadhipped type of figure, for this is the curse of glorious womanhood. Diagonal lines that start in a point near the neck and trek outwards towards the widest part of you are sure disaster. You can just as well choose a pattern with diagonal lines starting out at the point of the shoulder and coming in towards the tummy, but lots of people haven't found out that this is just as smart as the other. People who are nice and flat in the rear should play up this feature, for it is rare, but only these can dare dresses that cut in just a little above and below the—shall we say posterior?—and get away with it. Others, not so fortunate, may affect dresses that come down close to the waistline in back and flare below; they may go in for jackets or—and this is best of all—for little cape backs, boleros or judicious blousing that will play down their defect. You mustn't put bows upon your hip-bones or where you sit down.

Smart tricks to hide those generous hips

If this type of figure is exaggerated into the Spanish type, which is tiny above the waist and capacious below, picture frocks for evening become poems, veritable poems of delight. You know perfectly well that telephone dolls look as if they were tiny all the way down, which is the impression that modern women like to create. But very large women, on Junoesque lines, often have the fond and mistaken idea that robes de style are slenderizing. Many a dinner guest has had premature indigestion caused by the sight of a hostess barging down on him, all taffeta folds and terrifying bulk.

Truths about robes de style

For you who are not slim

Large women have many mistaken ideas that are cheerfully encouraged by people who seem intent on making large women seem enormous, and plump ones fat. These ideas fall into three classifications: (1) that loosely fitted and flowing garments make the figure seem smaller (2) that skimpy and tightly fitted clothes make the figure seem smaller (3) that straight up-and-down lines always give a false impression of slimness. All of them, if taken too literally, are snares and delusions. The first two fall under the head of Fitting, which will be discussed later. The third must be dealt with at once.

Everyone knows about "those long, slender lines." No woman in her senses believes that horizontal stripes, flapper tuck-in blouses, or oriental girdles wrapped tightly around the hips are flattering to a buxom figure. But the classification forgets a very important thing. If a woman has one good line in her figure, this should be played up by all means. Many large women, for instance, have slim hips, but are lured into straight dresses that hang straight from the shoulder so that this desirable line is lost. They seldom remember the principle, already discussed, that a skirt flaring at the bottom and a cape effect at the shoulder makes the middle part of the body seem smaller.

Rediscovering the good lines

A bug-a-boo has also been created to the effect that the new lines, which emphasize the natural waist-line, are not for large women. It is true that only matchstick women, with hankerings for feminine curves, should essay Patouish evening gowns on nightdress lines with a high string belt tight around them. These exaggerate the curves above and below the belt and are extremely difficult to wear. But high waist-lines are not a matter of belts, necessarily. A slight suggestion of a curve inward on a longish dress will give the impression of slenderness there without the trying actuality of it. And lines that are carried up to the natural waist-line, even if the dress is not indented there at all, give a new impression.

Now about these normal waist-lines

There may be just a patch of vertical tucks or shirrings at the natural waist-line in front or at each side of the front that makes you forget that the actual waist-line is in the old familiar place. Diagonal lines, either set in the material or achieved by flounces or pieces of the fabric, may ascend to the top of the hip or above it at one side and suggest a waist-line without revealing it. Women with diaphragms that bulge are usually safest with all or part of the waist-line at the top of the hip, which is still smart and may be made to look new as well.

After all, nobody looks like a fashion illustration.

MAKING SMART CLOTHES
FLATTERY IN FABRICS

In the selection of fabrics to do full justice to the ravishing pattern you have picked out, it should be unnecessary to remind anyone never to buy anything but the very finest grade of material. Bargains in silks and woolens do not survive many trips to the cleaners gracefully; they tend to pull and fray at the seams and look shabby practically at once; they wrinkle terribly at the least provocation. Never skimp on material, even though you are crazy for remnant sales—buy the exact amount that the pattern calls for. It cannot be made to stretch, and this kind of economy always shows.

False economy is one of the cardinal sins

In general, remember that evening chiffons should not be made on tailored lines—chiffon was made to flutter. Heavy woolens should not be gathered; stiff materials are good for sudden poufs in the Boulanger manner but make you look enormous if draped. Your own good sense and experience should teach you this and every Butterick envelope offers suggestions for fabrics that will carry out the mood of the dress most successfully. It is wisest not to veer from these.

There's good advice on the new envelope

Materials that are luxurious in themselves, like velvets and metal cloths and brocaded or embroidered affairs should be made by patterns of suitable simplicity or they will entirely swamp you. They need little but careful fitting and their own intrinsic beauty to startle the world. Beautiful prints should not be cut up into little intricate piecings—you are likely to have hysterics when you start putting them together again and, besides, it will confuse the eye after it is accomplished. By the same token, figured materials are best for the beginner who is not yet sufficiently experienced to realize that dressmaking is easy; for dazzling fabrics conceal little slips due to early carelessness whereas they show up startlingly on plain goods.

Plain fabrics, like flat crêpes and romas need more intricate design to make them look important. And only a woman sure of her talents and capable of taking careful pains should essay a dress of flat crêpe to wear to the opera. Satins, also, must be handled very tenderly. Nothing is more beautiful than this fabric if it is well fitted and well handled; if not, the shiny surface tends to emphasize every curve and exaggerate it. Satin, as you must know, is not for women too heavily endowed with curves, anyway.

Satin snares the unwary

Little hints about prints In selecting prints, the large woman should remember a cardinal principle. Any fabric or combination of fabrics making the body seem to recede from the dress itself is slenderizing in effect. Bright small prints (all large woman know that splashy prints are almost inevitably fatal) on a dark ground, particularly those that look as if the design were raised on the body of the fabric in a three-dimensional way, make the figure look slimmer than the dress. Although loosely fitted clothes add to bulk and make it shapeless as well as huge, a dress with a carefully fitted slip and a fluttering overdress of sheer material will do the same thing for you. Large women, by the way, should not have the slip cut straight across the front but should have it built up on the shoulders, or they will look huge of shoulder.

Accessories should be seen but not heard The ensemble idea gives one a perfect opportunity to indulge a fancy for combining fabrics—and colors, too. The smart costume should be a symphony of line, texture and tone, carefully assembled.

A great deal of to-do has been made lately about color ensembles. If you go in for brilliant colors, be very careful not to use too much of them. A bright Kelly green dress usually looks more chic if only a touch of green in the ornament of a dark hat carries out the color scheme. Too much color distracts attention from the wearer's face and personality in general, and this is not a good idea.

Stockings and gloves should match exactly; your shoes should have some good relation to your handbag and jewellery should be carefully selected so that no confusion results from having an amethyst pin on the hat and a ruby necklace around the neck. Such bad matches (even if the jewels are real, they are bad together) are inexcusable in days when costume jewellery is both attractive and inexpensive. But try not to overdo your ensemble; if the hat, shoes, bag, dress, and coat lining are all of the same dizzy fabric, you are bound to look too thought-out and self conscious.

A successful ensemble is no accident Discreetly done, the ensemble idea will result in a reputation for good taste. For instance, as you proceed with your experience, a last year's coat may be relined, in a fabric and color to match the dress beneath. A bit of ribbon or a pin on that smart little hat will make it look as if it had been made to order for that particular dress.

MAKING SMART CLOTHES
CHARACTER IN COLORS

Everyone responds in some way to all colors and there are literally hundreds of colors in fabrics from which you may choose when you buy material for your next costume.

All people do not respond in the same way to colors. Speaking broadly, color produces two reactions upon people, namely: an exhilarating effect, the positive reaction, and a depressing effect, the negative reaction, with many degrees in between—from slight to strong reactions in each color group. Warm colors, the reds, yellows, some greens, and some red purples, may produce feelings ranging from a positive feeling of well-being and contentment to a feeling of violent excitement and a desire to go out and "get" something or somebody. *Try a little red for that tired feeling*

The cool colors, blues, blue-greens, violets, and some greens, may produce feeling ranging from calmness and security to a definite feeling of depression and inadequacy. *If you would be calm wear cool colors*

The strength of either kind of reaction is due not only to the warmth or coolness of the color but to the temperament of the individual who wears the color or who looks at it as well.

Since color is possessed with all this potential ability to give pleasure or pain, it is evident that an understanding of how it affects people is practically a necessity.

The colors you wear may be the greatest single aid or hindrance to your beauty. The color of your dress may completely defeat the well planned and well selected design. The color of your costume may make you alluring or insignificant.

Not only do people vary in the way they react to colors but there are no two people who have exactly the same combination of coloring of hair, eyes, and skin. Your facial expression and build must also be considered. In other words, no two personalities are alike in spite of a rather general belief in "types." The exact color of your skin, hair, and eyes, and the characteristics of your personality all must be taken into account in accurately determining which of the many colors are best for you. *Colors must accent your personality*

Many of us have acquired color habits. Some are good but most unnecessarily limit our color choices when we could select from a wide variety. You know the

For that "dark brown taste" woman who says, "I always wear brown". She may have worn brown very well as a young person but as a middle-aged woman her own coloring has changed in a number of ways and "her browns" may no longer be good; in fact they may be definitely detrimental to her appearance but she goes on wearing a restricted color range and looking badly dressed, and feeling a vague dissatisfaction with her clothes which she cannot analyze, all because she has that "dark brown taste".

How then shall we make a discriminating selection of colors for our clothes so that we may be reasonably sure of choosing the right ones?

Here are some general facts about color selection which will be a guide for you.

Do not think of yourself as a type. You probably have mixed color characteristics.

First, consider the color of your skin very carefully. More of it shows in your personal color harmony than any other feature in coloring.

Warm colors to vitalize your skin The object in wearing colors is to make one's skin look as vital and fresh as possible not only by means of color in the cheeks and lips but by suggesting vibration of healthy color in the throat or wherever the skin is exposed.

The colors which will do most to make skins look vital are certain reds, if not too bright, pale coral color, peach color, and flesh color with a warm cast.

For the rather fragile looking fair skinned person certain cool reds in middle and paler tones are apt to be good. The only people who must avoid the reds are those with florid coloring.

Another range of colors which vitalizes the skin is the blue-green range since they suggest an opposite color, red, which after all is the color we try to force up from under the skin.

Dark and medium blue-greens do wonderful things for skins. The only people who need to beware of blue-greens are those whose eyes are of a decidedly purple blue. Blue-greens will make their eyes look impersonal and steel-like. Intense jade green in large amounts makes a dark skin look too swarthy or a florid skin too coarse, but is very becoming to a honey color suntan skin.

For blonde or brunette or titian locks Hair coloring usually falls in the yellow, red or brown range, with some blond hair seeming to measure in a clear warm yellow path, presenting few color problems. Hair of the mouse colored, medium blond type calls for dark browns, navy blue, and dark reds in clothes, provided these colors are good with the person's skin and eyes. The person with medium blond hair seldom wears beige unless she is a vital personality with clear skin and sparkling eyes.

The middle-aged woman whose hair has started to get gray has a real color problem in dressing because of her hair. She must avoid anything which emphasizes the middle or mixed look, which is characteristic of her hair. As a rule she avoids medium shades, or middle values of all colors, selecting the dark or the light colors in her best color ranges, always providing her build is such that she can wear light colors successfully. **Medium shades are not for graying hair**

Black sometimes is very flattering to hair of this kind since it emphasizes the dark color still left in the hair and by contrast throws into relief the gray portions forming gleaming silver high lights. This makes an otherwise dull mixed head of hair begin to sparkle in a subdued way which is very distinguished.

Browns are usually trying for hair of the mixed kind. Black and white tweeds, while good in coats, are apt to be poor for dresses when the hat is removed and the hair shows. Select either red, green, blue-green, or warm purple tweed mixtures.

The white haired woman has a much easier time selecting the right colors. Any color that throws her hair in relief will be flattering, with the possible exception of brown, although the brown eyed, clear skinned, white haired woman looks rather well in brown velvet and brown furs. She does not wear beige in sweaters or hats as well as she does colors with more depth and clearness. **But white hair presents few real problems**

Gray flatters her hair provided it tones to the same kind of gray as her hair does and provided her skin is clear enough to stand the rather chilling effect of gray worn near the face.

Eye coloring is more subtle but more sparkling than the other factors making up personal color harmony. We used to be told to dress in a color which was becoming to the eyes and all would be well. Now we know that the color we wear must be becoming first of all to the skin and then to the eyes and hair as well. **Your eyes are the court of last resort**

The colors we wear should add to the apparent depth and sympathetic expression of the eyes. Eyes are often mixed in color. That is, a brown eye often has certain dull yellow lights as well as dark yellow-red lights in it, while a so called blue eye may be either purple-blue, blue, or blue-green. So called hazel eyes often are chiefly yellow-green.

This color variation within the eye itself makes it possible, often, for one to deepen its color by wearing either of two or sometimes three colors and is the reason a woman almost always finds after thoroughly diagnosing herself, that her range of wearable colors has been increased to a surprising degree.

Brown, reds, greens will all deepen the color of brown eyes.

Brown or blue or hazel — the "eyes" have it

Blue eyes will be deepened by the blue, purple-blue, or blue-green which most nearly matches the eye color. The color in so called blue eyes is more often rendered weak and uninteresting by the use of an "off blue" for the given blue eye than by any other factor.

Hazel eyes are fascinating to dress since by the selection of yellow greens hazel eyes can be made to give an amber light and a surprisingly alluring expression, while warm red-purples will make hazel eyes glow with a remarkably intriguing green glow.

Of course you can wear black

This question often arises: "Can I wear black?" Almost anyone can wear black in some texture but not everyone can wear black in all textures. For some skins black should be worn with a transition color between the black fabric and the skin. This is true when the skin is of a china-like transparency and rather colorless. It is also true when a skin is inclined to be sallow. The flattering colors which make black becoming to people with these two kinds of skins are warm flesh color, egg shell and soft very pale pinks. Old ivory in the textures one finds in laces and net is flattering to almost any skin.

Black flat crepe is a little more trying than a canton crepe or a crepe with some sparkle in its weave. Satin is trying for the heavy figure but many women can wear black satin who would find satin in strong colors very unflattering for their build and ageing for their skins.

Black in transparent and semi-transparent textures such as chiffon, crepe Roma, georgette, etc., is apt to be becoming to a very great many women.

Black taffeta, if very stiff, has a tendency to produce an austere effect or may even age a woman whose skin needs to be made softer and more glowing. Black taffeta is on the contrary very becoming to youthful faces and figures and is usually used for the bouffant costume for afternoon or evening wear.

Black has a tendency to make figures appear slimmer and where the lines of the costume are long and sweeping this color adds inches to the height to the figure.

If you must wear white, wear "off white"

Many women are apprehensive concerning the becomingness of white, and this is quite as it should be. A dead white is trying to all but the most perfect skins as well as adding to the apparent size of the figure. "Off white" tones on the contrary are apt to be flattering to women of many ages and colorings.

Pastels are frequently flattering

The pale slightly grayed pastel colors such as flesh color, Vionnet pink, egg-shell, pale orchid, coral, pale blue greens and very pale warm yellow reds, old ivory, etc., often have the effect of clarifying a somewhat sallow skin. It is necessary to experiment with these colors held near the skin to determine which of the off white shades are best for you. In general the gleam of satin in these colors is trying to many skins but the same color in crepe and chiffon is often very flattering.

A few cautions seem to be necessary concerning color selections. For instance, a strong bright purple-blue is very trying to a great many skins. This is a real note of warning since the color itself seems to have a great appeal and is often selected because the woman or her husband "likes blue".

It seems that purples are very difficult

This strong deep purple-blue calls forth all the lurking yellow which may be an underlying color in many skins and so produces almost brownish shadows in the hollow parts of the face and neck contours.

There are two kinds of people who wear this bright purple-blue best. One is the clear skinned woman with purple-blue eyes and honey colored or spun gold hair. The other is the woman with fair peaches and cream skin, snappy brown eyes, and black hair. In both cases the personality should be the strong vital type.

A word concerning purples. Contrary to the generally accepted belief purples are rather difficult to use in clothes. Purple is supposed to be a good color for the matronly type or for the elderly woman. Most purples have a tendency to make the skin look either fragile or sallow. Certain warm purple reds such as an egg plant color, however, do wonderful things to clear and vitalize certain skins, particularly skins which have lost their first freshness.

The strong royal purple is a difficult color for almost anyone to wear.

There have been seasons when it was fashionable to appear heavily sun tanned, if not swarthy. The younger set have used the strong purple-blue and the rather harsh bright red-purple to enhance this heavily tanned effect. Both colors, however, have the effect of making the skin appear coarse, to say nothing of what they may do to dim the brightness of the eyes.

Fashion in colors is all important. Every season certain colors receive favorable fashion acceptance. There are usually enough of these fashion-right colors to make it entirely possible to supply a large range of color choice in selecting colors for clothes which are also one's becoming colors. However nothing is gained by wearing a fashion-right color if the color is unflattering for one's hair, eyes, or skin.

Last, but not least, colors must also be fashion right

MAKING SMART CLOTHES
SAFE SHOPPING GUIDES

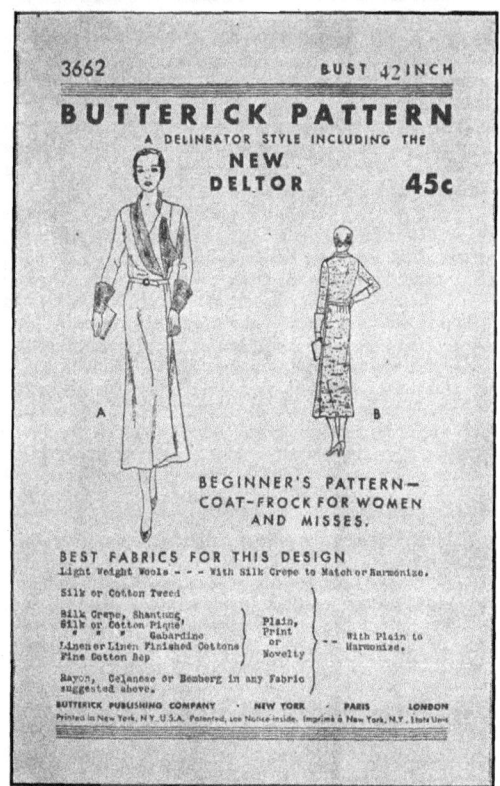

1. The guide to fashion-right fabrics   One of the many helpful services offered by every Butterick pattern is the shopping guide for fabrics on the front of the pattern envelope.

Here listed according to view are all the fabrics that successfully interpret the spirit of the design. These lists are made up after actual experiments by expert dressmakers have demonstrated what fabrics will insure perfection for the smart lines visualized by the designer.

ALL BUTTERICK FABRIC QUANTITIES GUARANTEED

On the reverse side of every Butterick pattern envelope you will find that other important shopping service—the chart of fabric quantities. You will find exactly how many yards of fabric you must buy for your exact size in every width in which the recommended fabrics come. These fabric quantities, of course, are for the figure of average height. Consult the "finished back length" measure which you will find at the top of your fabric chart. This will tell you just how many inches your garment will measure from neckline to finished hem and what hem allowance the pattern makes.

2. The chart of guaranteed quantities

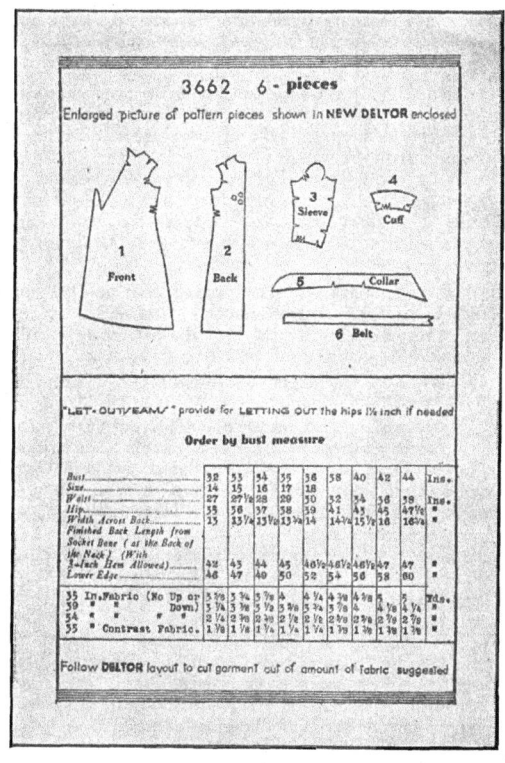

MAKING SMART CLOTHES
PATTERN ADJUSTMENT

You might just as well have the right size

Now that you know just what colors and fabrics were made in heaven for you and now that you've found the pattern of your dreams, don't think you're through. You must be sure that the size you think you want is the size that does you justice. People who buy ready-made clothes are often deluded into thinking they are a size fourteen, just because some manufacturer happens to make them large to flatter his customers. And then, too, the individual idiosyncrasies of your figure must be considered. No sizing, even though it is as carefully worked out as in Butterick patterns can completely allow for abnormally fat arms for instance on a size sixteen chassis. The only way to be really sure is to insist on being measured.

Your pattern envelope saves your pennies

Then armed with your pattern in the right size you will be fully equipped to cope with those big bewildering fabric displays for the shopping service on your pattern envelope will lead you by the hand. On the front there is a list of the fabrics in which your design looks best (and you can't improve on it). On the back there is a chart that tells you exactly how many yards to buy in what width and it certainly saves your pennies.

Naturally, once you have lugged your new pattern and the right amount of material home with you, the next thing is to be assured that the pattern is exactly the right length for you. By holding the paper pattern up against you, you can decide for yourself how you want to work it out.

Your waistline, for instance, must fall at exactly the right point and this business of adjusting your pattern to your figure before ever you start to cut your cherished fabric was especially invented to save you grey hairs. By the simple little trick of pinning your pattern pieces carefully together and trying this half garment on you are saved all the anguish of discovering when it is much too late, that your waistline has wandered several inches from its scheduled moorings or that by hemming according to Hoyle you will practically eliminate the plaits. And unless you know for sure that the "finished back length" specification which you'll find on your pattern envelope is the right "finished back length" for you, you'll seize this opportunity to settle the hemline question.

EVERY PATTERN MARKING HAS A STYLE MEANING

When you are ready to start the making of your garment, take the pattern from the envelope; lay aside for a moment the Deltor, which is enclosed with every Butterick pattern, and spread out the pattern pieces. Note on the front of the envelope the "view" you have decided to make; then turn to the back of the envelope or the Deltor chart of pattern pieces to see if there are any that you will not need, as, for instance, the sleeve pattern, if you are making the sleeveless version. If there are, put them back into the envelope, so that they will not be in your way.

On most pattern pieces you will find notches and perforations. Every notch and every perforation has been made to help you either in the cutting or construction of your garment.

Some of the perforations appear in almost every Butterick pattern. Among these are two small ones, placed horizontally, that say to you "this is the location of the natural waistline in a figure of average proportions." Take note of these, for they will help you to find out whether you vary from the average in waist length, a most important point to determine before you cut out your garment. Sometimes these same little perforations are used on the sleeve to mark the elbow.

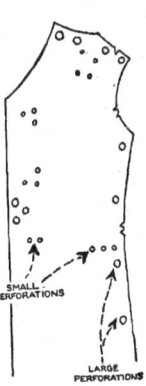

3. Perforations tell you the whole story

Other perforations that soon become familiar to a user of Butterick patterns are three large ones, grouped in triangular form, which mark an edge that must be placed on a fold of the material; a row of large ones, in groups of two, indicating a line that must be laid on the grain of the material; and a very important line of large perforations running along some edges, three-quarters of an inch back from the edge. These mark the let-out seam, which Butterick patterns provide to take care of any slight variations from the average which your measurements may show. It is by the use of such a seam that the great couturiers of Paris mould their garments to the figures of their clients and attain that perfection of line which marks the made-to-measure frock.

There are other perforations, both large and small, showing how to handle special details of construction —where to lay plaits, make shirrings, insert panels, etc. Specific directions for using these perforations and for matching notches are given by printed word and by illustration in the Deltor.

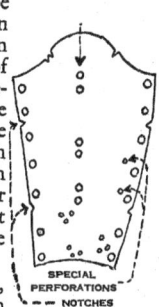

4. Notches and special marks have a purpose

TALL AND SHORT FIGURES CAN BE EQUALLY CHIC

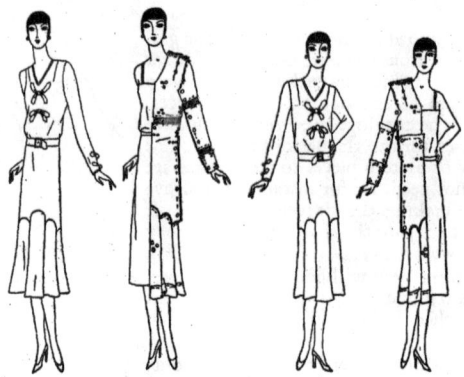

5. Alterations in the waist and sleeve for tall figures

6. But if you're short you do it like this, pinning tucks

By the help of the let-out seams, you can usually do any necessary adjusting after your garment is cut and basted, but there are a few cases in which the pattern itself should be altered before the material is cut.

The first of these occurs when you are taller or shorter than the average. The easiest and best way to test this is to pin the pattern together and slip it on (illustrations 5 and 6), leaving a few inches unpinned at the top of the underarm and sleeve seams to avoid tearing the pattern.

Two small perforations mark the waistline

Find the two small perforations marking the natural waistline, both front and back, and see whether they come exactly at your natural waistline. If they do, the pattern is correct for you in that respect. If they come below your waistline, pin a tuck in the bodice of the pattern as shown in illustration 7. If they come above your waistline, measure to see how much above, and take the pattern off. Cut it across a few inches above the perforations; separate the cut edges as much as necessary, and pin a strip of paper underneath to hold them in place, then try the pattern on again before unpinning the seams (illustration 5).

Sleeves are altered in length in the same way.

The Deltor shows you where such alterations should be made in order to keep the good lines of the garment which it accompanies.

LENGTH OF PATTERN ADJUSTED BEFORE CUTTING

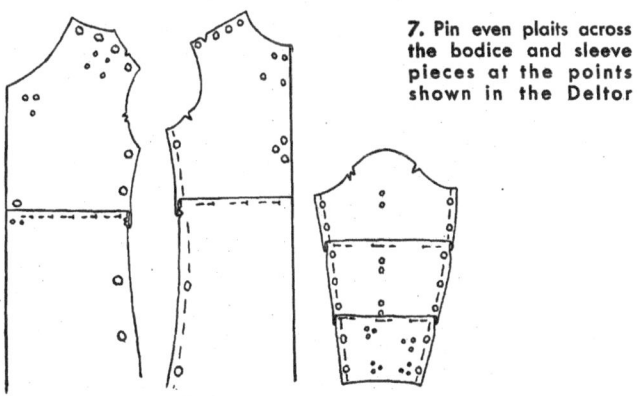

7. Pin even plaits across the bodice and sleeve pieces at the points shown in the Deltor

FOR THE FIGURE SHORTER THAN NORMAL

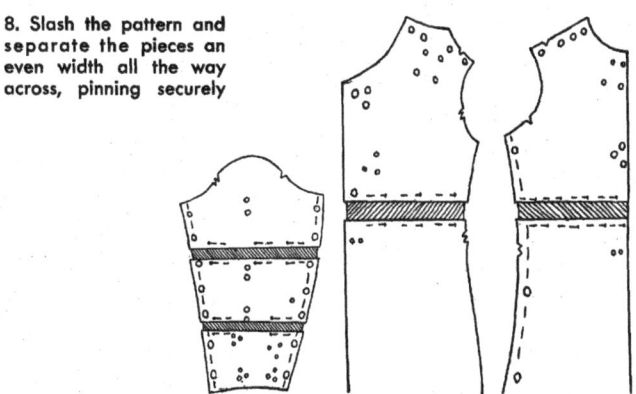

8. Slash the pattern and separate the pieces an even width all the way across, pinning securely

FOR THE FIGURE TALLER THAN NORMAL

FLARES AND FLOUNCES MERIT SPECIAL MENTION

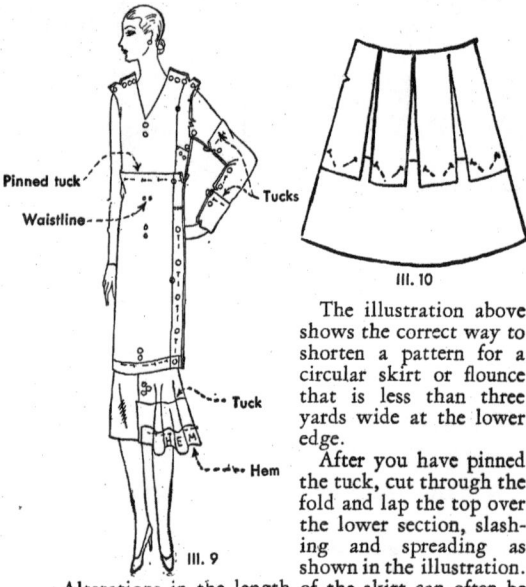

Ill. 10

Ill. 9

The illustration above shows the correct way to shorten a pattern for a circular skirt or flounce that is less than three yards wide at the lower edge.

After you have pinned the tuck, cut through the fold and lap the top over the lower section, slashing and spreading as shown in the illustration.

It's very easy to pin a tuck

Alterations in the length of the skirt can often be made by adding to or taking away from the bottom, but in some cases this would be disastrous to the lines of the garment.

For instance, in the frock shown on this page, you see that the pattern may be lengthened by adding to the bottom of the circular flounce, but if the skirt must be shortened, the length should be taken out by making a tuck through the middle of the flounce.

The reason the Deltor for this pattern tells you to do your shortening here is that the flounce is not a very full circular design and if you cut a strip from the bottom, it will take away too much from the ripple.

Attention to details of this kind is one of the exclusive and valuable features of the Deltors that are made for Butterick patterns. By reading and following the suggestions given in the Deltor you are using, you will be sure of a perfectly fitting frock.

SIMPLE ALTERATIONS FOR EVES OF VARIOUS AGES

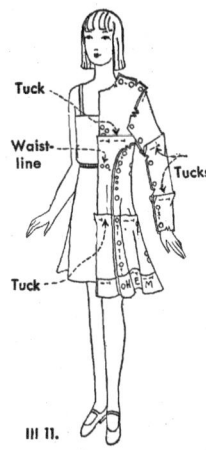

Ill 11.

No matter how young she may be, any little girl likes pretty clothes, and just as much care is given to making Butterick patterns and Deltors for children as for their mothers. Children's patterns ought to be as carefully tested for length as those of an adult, and any necessary alterations should be made, before cutting, at the points illustrated in the Deltor.

The dress that is to be made for this little girl would lose the chic effect of its flare if the set-in panel were shortened or lengthened at the hem, so the Deltor says that the place to lengthen or shorten it is a little below the hip.

11. Where to snip and when to take a tuck

Nowhere does skill and experience in creating a design show more clearly than in a flounce, especially a circular flounce, where so much depends upon having just the required amount of fullness, and having the ripples fall in the right places.

The Deltor says that the flounces on this dress may be either lengthened or shortened at the bottom. That is because these flounces are very full and the effect will not be spoiled by adding to or taking from the lower edge. By consulting your Deltor and following its suggestions, you will always be sure of success.

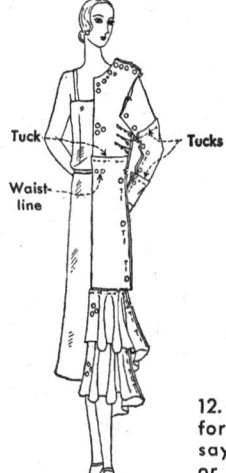

12. The Deltor for this design says lengthen or shorten at edge of flounce

ACCOMMODATING THAT TOO TOO SOLID FLESH

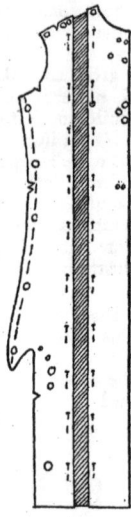 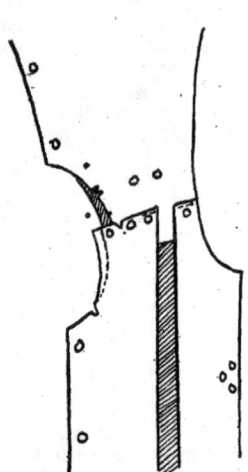

13. Back cut and widened evenly all the way down

14. Building out front to accommodate the widened back

In addition to the alterations which must be made in the length of patterns to adjust them to tall or short figures, the varying weights of figures of the same height sometimes necessitate other alterations which though simple to make mean much to the comfort and smartness of the finished frock.

For a back that is broad in proportion to the front breadth of the figure, the pattern should be altered before the material is cut. Slash the back straight down and spread apart as much as necessary, pinning a strip of paper underneath to hold edges in place. (Ill. 13)

This will make the back shoulder edge wider than the front. To correct the line, place the edges together and adjust as in illustration 14, cutting one half of the excess from the back and building out the front to meet it, letting both alterations run to nothing at notches.

A CALL TO ARMS—
ESPECIALLY LARGE ONES

Nothing is more important to the success of your frock than sleeves that fit easily, especially if your arms are a little larger than the average. It is so easy to avoid that ugly pull across the top of your sleeve by altering your pattern before you even begin to cut your fabric.

An arm that is only a little fuller than the average is easily fitted by the help of the let-out seam, but under no circumstances should there be any skimping at this seam.

For an arm considerably larger than the average, over its full length, cut the sleeve pattern down from the top almost to the bottom and separate the edges as shown in illustration 15.

For an arm that is large in the muscular section between elbow and shoulder, lay the sleeve pattern on a fresh piece of paper, outline the top; then slash a little in back of the center and spread the pattern as in illustration 16. Lay darts to take up the resulting fullness and build the top up to the outline you drew.

If the arm is consistently large above the elbow, make the necessary adjustment by cutting and spreading the pattern as in illustration 17. When a sleeve pattern is widened at the top by either of these methods, it will be necessary to shape the top to follow the original line and to slash the armhole slightly to take in the enlarged sleeve.

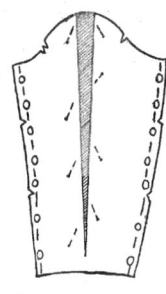

15. For arm larger than average over full length

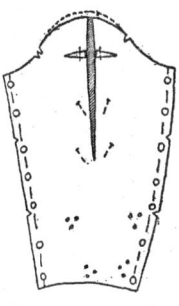

16. For arm with the athletic muscle

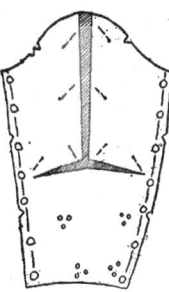

17. For arm consistently large above the elbow

MAKING SMART CLOTHES
MODERN METHODS OF CUTTING

If you've ever been condemned to wear a frock with a skirt that ripples gently in all the wrong places or sleeves that twine insistently about your arms then we needn't seek to impress you further with the gravity of this cutting situation. It is indeed a situation worthy of your best intelligence, for as much perfectly grand material has been mangled in the cutting as has been made into smart frocks, and so unnecessarily too, as you well know, if you've ever seen the cutting layouts that **Why experiment** come with every Butterick Pattern. The secret of cor-
when Butterick rect cutting which is actually the foundation of smart-
does it for you ness in any garment is simple enough, when you can follow the directions that have been worked out for you by experts. Of course, if you're going to insist on experimenting with your hard-earned fabric that's your affair, but it is only kind to warn you that you are going to run into difficulties of which the very least will be a shortage of material. It seems hardly necessary to paint a picture of all the other horrors that lurk around dark corners for the inexperienced.

Tucked just inside the flap of your Butterick Pattern
The Deltor is envelope is a working blueprint of the design you have
your working chosen. This is the famous Deltor, exclusive with
blue print Butterick, which gives you complete directions for cutting, putting together and finishing your frock. Comprehensive cutting layouts as accurate as an architect's blueprint are a patented feature of this Deltor. These simple cutting guides eliminate every vestige of the "cutting problem" from your home dressmaking. They are scientifically planned to cut your garment from the exact amount of yardage listed on the pattern envelope. They demonstrate exactly how to place pattern pieces most advantageously on this amount of material ... pattern pieces in your exact size on the width of fabric you have purchased for every Deltor shows a
Comprehen- separate guide for cutting every view shown on the pat-
sive layouts tern envelope in every size in which the pattern is made
for cutting from every width of material recommended.

The reverse side of this remarkable instruction sheet demonstrates in simple pictures and explanatory text exactly how to put your frock together step-by-step and finish it with the same finesse of the smart original. The Deltor is Butterick's own prescription for successful dressmaking.

THE NEW DELTOR ANSWERS EVERY CUTTING QUESTION

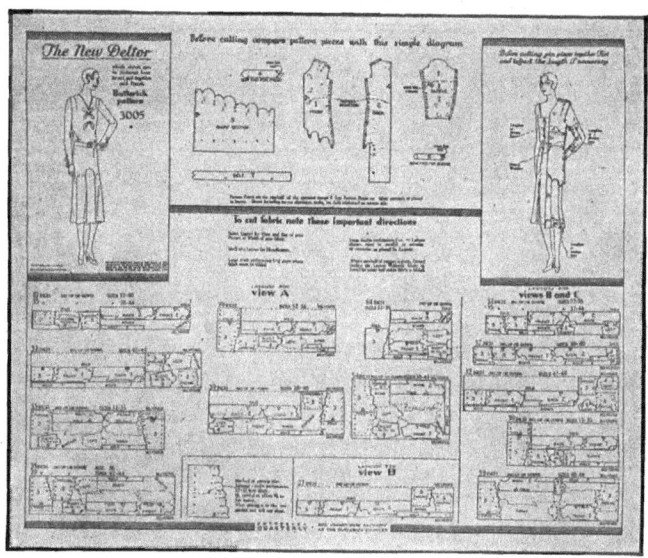

18. Every view in every size for every width of material

When a pattern is given to a cutter, he lays it out just as though he were preparing to cut a garment. Carefully and skilfully he fits the pieces on. Suppose the recommended materials come in a wide range of widths —say twenty-seven, thirty-five, thirty-nine, and fifty-four inches. The cutter must lay the pattern out on every one of these widths. *Experienced cutters plan these layouts*

Perhaps he finds that the garment can not be cut economically, or requires too much piecing, or piecing in the wrong places, if cut from twenty-seven-inch material. That width is, therefore, not recommended, and is omitted from the table of required quantities printed on the pattern envelope. But in thirty-five-inch material a good layout can be made, and that is one of those listed.

The cutter is given all the time he needs to work over his layout, because sometimes even the most skilful cutter can, by trying the pieces in various positions, work out a more economical layout than appeared possible at

CUT TO ADVANTAGE
FOLLOW THE DELTOR

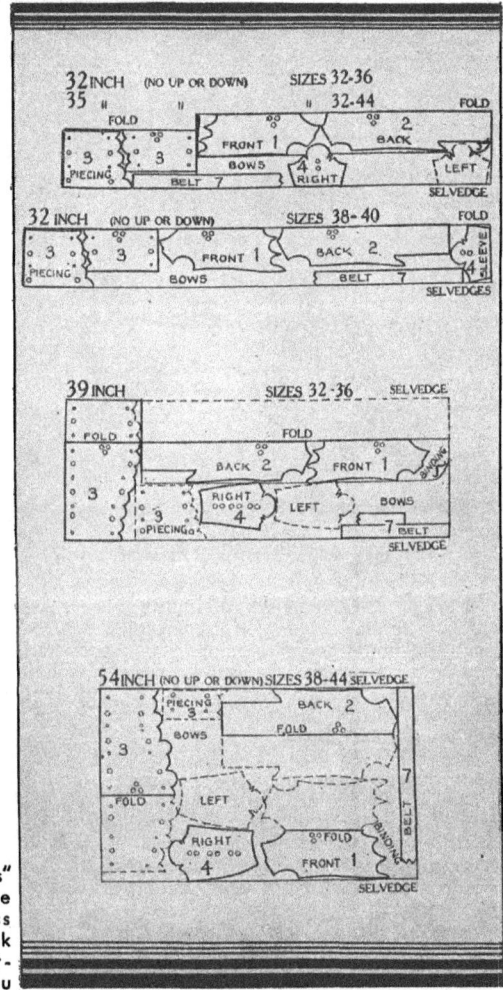

19. Four "lays" that show the completeness of Butterick cutting services to you

MAKE EVERY INCH COUNT
AND DON'T RUN SHORT

first; and by spending this time he saves you the necessity of doing it.

After the layout is O. K.'d, an artist makes an exact copy of the arrangement of the pieces, and the layout that is given on the Deltor is made directly from this so that you can simply follow the picture of this expert cutter's layout in cutting your own garment.

This is only one step in the making of a Butterick Pattern, but it shows you why you are safe in depending upon the directions and diagrams that are furnished, because every other step is taken just as thoroughly. **You can depend on the diagrams**

The Deltor that is shown on page 25 is, of course, greatly reduced. The separate layouts on page 26, however, are just the size that they are in the Deltor. You can see how easy it is to follow them and how it saves you all the trouble of trying your pattern in various ways on your material.

In addition to saving you all the necessity of experimenting, the Deltor cutting layouts save you from the possibility of mistake in cutting your material. Such trying errors as cutting two sleeves for one arm can never occur if you place your pattern on the material just as it is placed in the Deltor layout you are following. If you have any doubt about the placing of a piece, such as a sleeve, that looks alike on two sides, you will see that the notches are reproduced for your guidance in this particular. Notice, too, that in each layout a piece of material is provided from which the bows for the front of the frock can be cut.

The side of the Deltor that you need at this point is the same one that helped you in checking the length of the pattern. It is the side with these cutting layouts. Spread it out and find the layout you need for the view you have chosen, in the size of your pattern, and for material of the width you have bought. Suppose, for instance, you are going to make, in View A, the dress for which the Deltor is given on page 25; that your size is 36, and that you have bought the quantity of 39 inch material listed on the pattern envelope as necessary for that view in size 36. The layout you need, in this case, is the one that is centered in the Deltor. (Ill. 19.) **Mark your layout with a circle for identification**

When you have found your layout, be sure to mark a heavy pencil line around it so that your eye will find it immediately whenever you look at your Deltor.

KEEP YOUR BLUEPRINT BEFORE YOU AS YOU WORK

Place your Deltor, with the cutting-layout side up, where you can see it easily but where it will not interfere with your work; then open out your material. It should be free from wrinkles, and if it is of a kind that needs sponging, that should have been done.

Measure it to see that it is correct both in width and length, and make sure that both ends are cut on a straight crosswise grain. (See page 30 for explanation of "grain.")

Watch for the grain of the fabric
Mention was made on page 17 of the perforations that show the grain line. This line is usually placed on the lengthwise grain of the material, but sometimes it is laid crosswise or on the bias. The Deltor layout shows you how it is to be laid in the garment you are cutting.

This matter of "grain" is of great importance in laying out your pattern pieces. In most cases when a sleeve twists or a circular flare hangs in deeper ripples on one side than on the other it is because the grain of the material was not followed carefully in the cutting.

Starting with one end of your cloth, stretch it smoothly along the length of the table, working from left to right. Hold it in place by laying small weights at the corners or at intervals along the edges.

Lay material right side up with care
If the material has a right and a wrong side, be sure that it is laid with the right side up. This is most important in cutting a design with a one-sided effect, as the layouts are planned so that each piece of the garment will be for the correct side of the body when the pattern pieces are arranged on the right side of the material as shown in the layout.

If your material has a distinct up and down your layout should show all the pieces of the pattern laid in the same direction on the fabric.

If the layout calls for a fold in the center of the material, fold one side over the other and pin the end together from the selvedges to the center, placing pins about six inches apart. Starting at the corner, pin the selvedges together at intervals of six inches, taking care not to hold any fullness in either edge. Lay the folded material flat on the table and, with the flat of your hand, smooth the material from selvedge to center, pinning the center fold every six inches.

FINDING THE FOLD IS A LESSON IN GEOMETRY

If the layout shows a fold that is not in the center, measure the widest part of the pattern piece that is to be cut from the folded section, and put a pin in your tape measure to mark this distance. Then measure the space marked, from the selvedge toward the center, at intervals of twelve inches, putting in pins to mark the line in the cloth. Fold the material along these pins and pin the fold to position as described above.

Use sharp, fine pins for this purpose, and also for pinning your pattern to the material. Heavy pins may scar or even make holes in fine material.

All pins, except those used in marking the line at which a fold is to be made, should be placed at right angles to the edge or fold that is being pinned.

Arrange your pattern on the material as shown in the Deltor layout which you have marked, and pin each piece to position. Start at the left and work toward the right, following the layout exactly. Each piece serves as a guide to the position of the next.

When a pattern piece is laid on a fold, pin the edge which lies along the fold first. In pinning on a piece that is not laid on a fold, be sure that the perforations marking the grain line follow the grain as shown in the layout.

Don't spare the pins; pin everything

THE GRAIN OF THE GOODS IS YOUR GUIDE TO CHIC

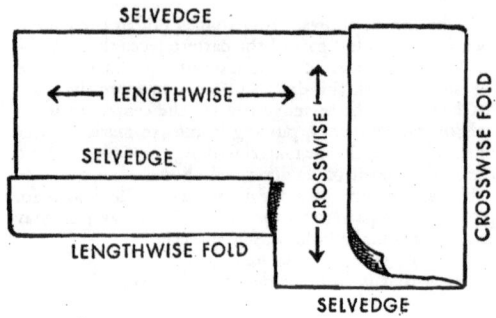

20. How to find the exact position of folds

The word "grain" used in connection with a fabric means the direction in which threads run. A lengthwise grain is one that follows a lengthwise, or warp, thread. A crosswise grain follows a weft or woof thread, running directly across the material from selvedge to selvedge. A bias grain cuts diagonally across the lengthwise and crosswise threads. It is important that whatever grain is being followed should be followed exactly, as it is the starting point for all designing and cutting.

Anyone who works with fabrics soon develops a good "sense" of grain, and an experienced dressmaker could not bring herself to cut without considering it; but beginners sometimes, either from carelessness or because they think they can economize by doing so, lay a sleeve or other section of the pattern just off the true, often with results so pathetic that the garment is practically unwearable, because the sleeve seam runs in a crooked line, or one side of the skirt sags and the other pulls up; and no amount of ripping and rebasting can ever make it just right.

The only way to be sure of getting a perfectly straight lengthwise or crosswise grain is to follow a thread. In materials where the threads are visible, this can be done by the eye.

If a thread can be pulled, either lengthwise or crosswise, this will give a true grain. Or course, threads must not be pulled out of fabric from which a garment

FINDING THE TRUE BIAS IS ANOTHER TRIANGLE CASE

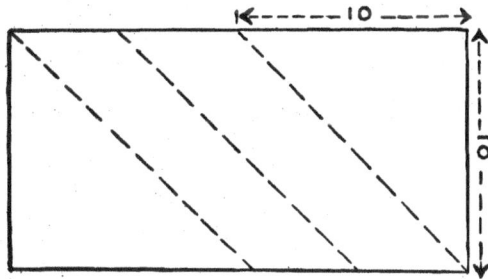

is to be cut, but it is often a quick way of straightening the end of a piece of material.

21. Let's get this straight

Where neither of these methods can be followed, a lengthwise grain can be found by measuring the same distance in from either selvedge at intervals of ten or twelve inches and inserting a row of pins to mark the line.

A straight grain, either lengthwise or crosswise, may be found fairly accurately by feeling. Fold the fabrics over in a straight line and pull the fold gently with your hands. If the pull feels stretchy and uneven, shift the fold until you get the effect of a straight, firm line from hand to hand, and pin this fold. Then move the hands along and get a straight line on the next section, until you have the fold pinned as far as required.

Sometimes, after you have found your crosswise grain you will see that it does not run quite straight across the material. This is probably because the fabric has been stretched a little crooked in the pressing and folding or rolling before it left the mill. In such a case, pull and stretch it gently until each crosswise thread makes a perfect right angle with both selvedges.

To find a true bias, cut one end of the material on a true crosswise grain; measure from the corner an equal distance (seven or eight inches is a good length) down the selvedge and across the end; mark with pins or a pencil; lay a yardstick diagonally across the material, touching both marks, and draw a line with tailors' chalk or mark the line with pins or basting thread.

CUTTING PLAIDS, STRIPES AND BORDERED FABRICS

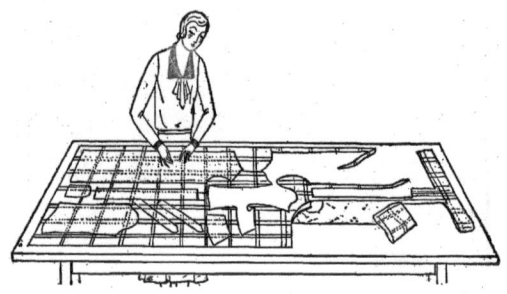

22. Match both lengthwise and crosswise stripes

In the cutting of stripes, plaids and bordered or figured materials, special care must be taken in matching the design so that when the garment is finished, there will not be that mixed-up appearance that is sometimes seen in a carelessly planned frock or coat made of material with a large, distinct design.

First, decide which stripe, plaid or figure is best for the center of the front and back. Place the front and the back on the material with the lower corners of the underarm edges the same distance below a crosswise stripe. Then lay the upper edge of the sleeve pattern on the front and back sections with the armhole notches matching, and, with a pencil, mark on the sleeve pattern the crosswise stripe nearest to the notches.

When the sleeve is laid on the material, lay the cuff pattern on it and mark the position of a stripe on the cuff pattern so the cuff can be cut to match the sleeve.

After cutting one front, one sleeve, one cuff, etc., lay **You must be sure to cut two of a kind** these pieces on the material with the right sides together, matching lengthwise and crosswise stripes, and cut the other half. Then lay the pattern on the cut sections of material again and mark the notches and perforations.

It must be borne in mind in laying out a pattern on an irregular plaid that all pieces of the pattern must be placed in the same direction on the material.

BUTTERICK PATTERNS HAVE CUT EDGES, READY TO USE

In cutting, use sharp, long shears, and follow the edge of the pattern exactly. If you use Butterick patterns there is no need to "allow for a seam." All seams are adequately provided for, and if you make any further allowance you will not only have a garment that is too large for you but you will also spoil its very carefully designed proportions.

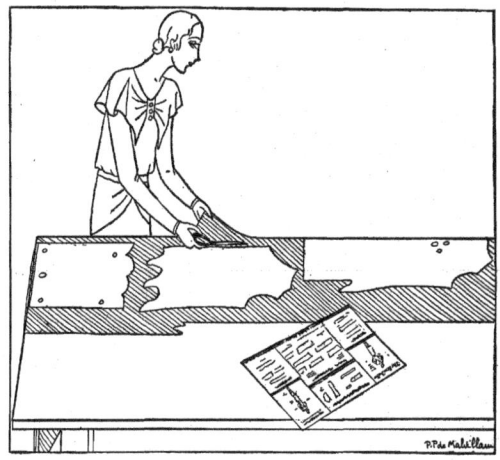

The only exception to this is when you are cutting a material that frays badly. In this case, allow an eighth of an inch on seams that do not have the line of perforations indicating a let-out seam. No allowance is needed on let-out seams, even when the material is of a kind that frays easily.

23. Cut right on edge of the pattern; there is no need to allow for seam

As soon as you have cut a garment from a loosely woven material, overcast the armhole and neck edges to prevent raveling.

Sometimes bias bindings, ruffles, flower petals, or other trimming and finishing pieces which do not require a pattern, are cut from pieces of material left over from the cutting of the main part of the garment. The Deltor layout shows where these may be cut to advantage in a professional manner.

NOTCHES AND PERFORATIONS
MARK THE WAY TO STYLE

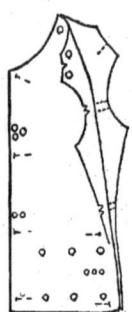

24. Notches marked by basting

Tailor's tacks will record every perforation on fabric

Before removing the pattern pieces from your material, mark every notch and every perforation that is to be used in putting the garment together. It is very important to mark the center front and center back lines with a line of uneven bastings. The perforations indicating grain line and those that show where a pattern edge is to be laid on a fold need not be marked.

The notches can be marked either with two or three stitches in basting cotton (illustration 24) or with small notches (not more than one-eighth inch deep) in the edge of the material. Marking with basting cotton is generally more satisfactory than notching.

The only really satisfactory way to mark the position of the different perforations is with tailor's tacks. To avoid confusion when putting the garment together, use one color of thread for small perforations and another for large ones.

Tailor's tacks are thread marks used to show on the material the locations of perforations in the pattern made while pattern is still on.

To make tailor's tacks, use a double thread, using one color of thread for small perforations and another color for large ones, without a knot. Take a stitch (or two stitches, one over the other) through each perforation, through both thicknesses of material if it is double. Where perforations are close together, as at the shoulder seam and waistline perforations in illustration 25, leave loops of thread between. Where perforations are more widely separated, just leave a loose stitch, as in the underarm seam illustrated.

Next cut the thread half way between the perforations and remove the pattern. If the material is double, separate the thicknesses a little and cut the thread between, leaving thread in each piece.

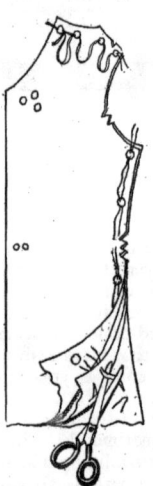

25. Clipping tailor's tacks

MAKING SMART CLOTHES
THE SCIENCE OF BASTING

When the pattern pieces have been unpinned and removed from the material, you are ready to begin the construction of your garment. Before machine stitching is done, the entire garment should be basted and and tried on.

In the first basting the stitches must run exactly along the line of perforations at all let-out seams (shoulder, underarm, sleeve, etc.). Then if there is any necessity for letting them out at any point they may be rebasted to fit.

Other seams should be basted three-eighths of an inch deep, except where an allowance of one-eighth of an inch has been made for easily frayed material.

seam allowances

On all edges of this pattern ⅜ in. (———) is allowed for seams and finishing.

let-out seams

On certain edges of this pattern an additional amount is allowed for letting out, if necessary. These edges are marked by lines of large single perforations O O   O Baste through the center of these perforations.

Baste together and try on. The frock should fit closely at hip.
If any slight alterations are necessary, they should be made before finishing is begun.

26. Watch the seams; read the Deltor

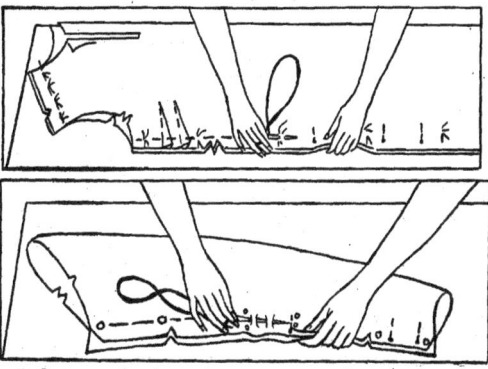

27. Baste thru tailor's tacks marking let-out seam on sleeve and bodice

Before you begin to baste, turn to the construction side of your Deltor and put the pieces together according to the printed directions and illustrations given.

35

PRELIMINARY BASTING WILL PREVENT RUEFUL RIPPING

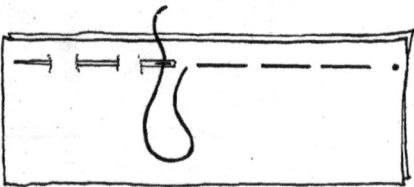

28. Even basting stitch

Careful basting is essential to good dressmaking. Even bastings are used for seams and other places where a considerable strain may come. Use a knot and make the stitches about one-fourth of an inch long on each side of the fabric, fastening off with double stitch.

29. Uneven basting

Uneven bastings differ from even bastings only in the relative length of the stitches on each side of the fabric. They can be put in more quickly than even bastings and are useful in places where there is not much strain, as in the first turning of a hem in testing the length of a garment, and to mark guide lines on frock.

30. Diagonal basting

Diagonal bastings are slanting stitches, used principally to secure the outside of a garment to its lining. They are especially useful when the lining is eased on to the material, because they make it possible to baste with loose stitches and still give sufficient hold so that there is no danger whatever of the fabric's slipping.

SMART BASTING TRICKS FOR SEAMS AND PLAITS

The usual type of set-in sleeve is always cut, in a Butterick pattern, so that it is a very little bit fuller than the armhole. This is necessary to prevent a puckering of the armhole. In basting in the sleeve, match the notches and pin together, then hold the sleeve toward you and baste from the sleeve side, easing in fullness across the top.

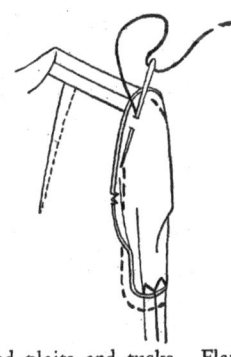

31. Basting in the sleeve

Firm, close, straight basting is essential for good plaits and tucks. Flat plaits are basted through three thicknesses of material. In basting a plaited skirt, where the seams have been stitched, slip a piece of cardboard inside to keep the needle from catching the other side.

Tucks are basted through only two thicknesses of material. The basting thread should run accurately along the line required for the depth of the tuck. To baste a curved tuck, mark the edge with tailor's tacks, page 34, or with pins. Fold the material on this line and if the tuck is a wide one, baste quite close to the edge. Then make another basting as far from the edge as the depth of the tuck required, holding and easing it in as you baste.

In basting silks and velvets, use a fine needle and silk thread, because a cotton thread often leaves a mark on such fabrics. When you are ready to take out your bastings, cut them every three or four inches. Pulling long basting threads from fine materials may mar or even tear the fabric.

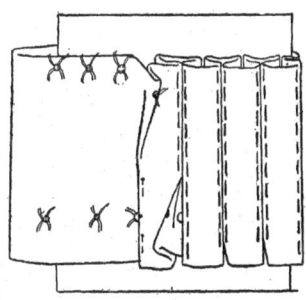

32. An easy method of basting plaits —using cardboard

TO MASTER SHARP POINTS AND MAKE SMOOTH CURVES

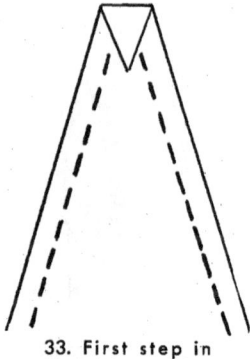

33. First step in finishing point

34. One edge turned in and trimmed at tip

Pointed and curved outlines must be handled with great care in order to insure fine, clean points and even curves.

When a pointed flounce or other section is to be basted inside a garment, pin the point at the top of the opening and pin the seams at intervals, being careful not to stretch either side. Then baste your seam, tapering it at the point. After the seam is stitched it may be turned in whatever direction you prefer and pressed flat.

When the point is to be applied to the outside of a garment, its edges must be turned in and basted. To get a fine, sharp point, turn the tip down first, then turn the side edges in, trimming them off at the top as much as necessary. (Ill. 33 and 34.)

Go slow on the curves

A circular edge that is carelessly turned in will make an unattractive outline, with a succession of points and straight lines instead of the smooth curve that is the result when the turning and basting are done properly. Baste near the turned edge with small stitches, and ease in the fullness of the circular edge evenly to fit the smaller circle over which it is turned.

It may be necessary to clip the seam allowance slightly to get a smooth edge.

MAKING SMART CLOTHES
MODERN METHODS OF FITTING

In no place do the shortcomings of the ordinary and misguided home dressmaker show up more radically than in the matter of fitting. Amateurs have a way of pulling a dress suddenly tight to show a good line (ignoring the bulge above and below) and then discovering afterwards that sitting down is practically impossible. Or else they follow the mealbag school and do not allow the dress for a minute to have the slightest contact with the body.

Clothes should fit closely, but never tightly in any one place. You know perfectly well what happens to an otherwise graceful pillow when you tie a string tight around it. Manage to get a mirror that makes it possible to view yourself in the rear—clothes pulled tight across this point not only make sitting down a real danger, but emphasize bulk. Look at yourself profile, too, and be sure that the dress fits perfectly over the hips and does not cut in unbecomingly above or below.

Clothes should fit closely but not too close

With all the smartest new frocks pinning their claims to fame and becomingness on a smooth unbroken line from the waist to well below the hips, any unexpected indentations are bound to be disastrous to your dreams of looking like a fashion illustration. Strange wrinkles never seen in any smart illustration are an easy way of checking up on the fit of your frock at this point. The sketches in the pages that follow will teach you how to recognize these tell-tale wrinkles and what to do about them.

•

This is the strategic moment for viewing your waistline with an impartial eye and making sure that your armholes are of a liberal size, so that the dress does not collapse at the armpits prematurely and make all your toil for nothing. Nothing, either, looks worse than a neckline that pulls out of place unless you anchor it firmly to your brassiere with a pin. Be sure that the dress is wide enough across the front so that the V, for instance, of the neck lies easily and gracefully upon you.

Confidential sessions at your mirror

By all means move around normally when you are fitting the dress so as to be certain that it will be graceful in motion as well as standing still.

Of course, you must always fit a dress wearing a girdle and underwear of the type that are eventually to be worn beneath it. A dress fitted with a girdle and worn without one develops surprising tricks.

FITTING THE FIGURE WITH LARGE HIPS

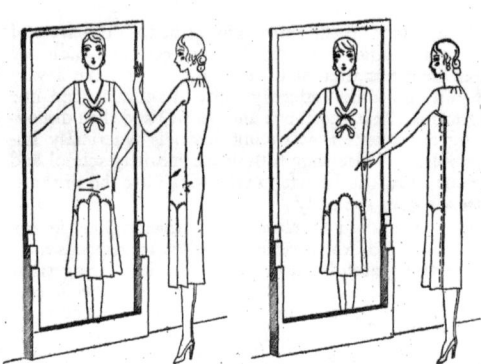

35. Large hips make Frocks appear tight; let-out seams quickly come to the rescue

After basting the main parts of your garment together, put it on and look it over carefully. Study it from all points, front, back, length, hang of skirt, fit of sleeve, whether it is too tight or too loose in any part, and whether there are any wrinkles that need to be eliminated. If any adjustment is necessary, decide what alterations need to be made before you begin to make any; then pin, rebaste, and try the garment on once more to be sure that everything is right before you do the permanent sewing.

One of the adjustments often necessary is the easing of a garment when the hips of the wearer are slightly larger than the average. In a case of this sort, the garment will form little wrinkles across the back and will draw in an ugly line in the back below the hips.

With the let-out seam, which Butterick patterns provide for just such contingencies, this is easily remedied. Baste the let-out seam, which was basted three-quarters of an inch deep originally, nearer the edge, letting out just enough to make the garment hang properly. The seam should be let out an equal amount all the way down from the hip to the lower edge, the alteration tapering to nothing above the hip.

Don't stop at the hipline

This will make a smooth seam and prevent any bulging or drawing where the alteration was made.

FITTING THE FIGURE WITH LARGE HIPS

An inch or two at the hips makes a difference in buying the pattern

If your hip measure is more than an inch and a half larger than the average, in comparison with your bust, it is better on the whole to make an exception to the rule that patterns should be bought by bust measure, and buy your pattern by hip measure. This will make the garment too long in the shoulder for you and a little large in the bust. To correct this, baste the garment as directed by the Deltor accompanying the pattern and try it on. Stand before the mirror and give the effect a thorough examination and decide on an armhole line that will flatter you most.

For the usual set-in sleeve, the joining of the sleeve to the body should come at the turn or round of the shoulders. Stick a pin where you feel the sleeve joining should come, leaving the shoulder as long as is most becoming for you.

36. Marking a becoming shoulder line

A figure with large hips will look more balanced in a dress fitted somewhat loosely across the shoulders and bust, so do not take more off the shoulder and bust than is essential. Having marked the place where you feel the sleeve joining should come, take the garment off, rip the shoulder seam and the side seams from the top as far down as the hips, lay the pattern pieces for the front and back of the waist on the material, as shown in illustration 37, and cut the material along the outlines of the pattern. If you feel nervous about cutting the material, mark the outlines with tailor's tacks, rebaste along these lines, and try the frock on again before trimming off the excess material.

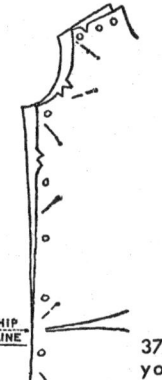

37. Correcting your pattern at shoulder

FITTING THE FIGURE WITH A LARGE BUST

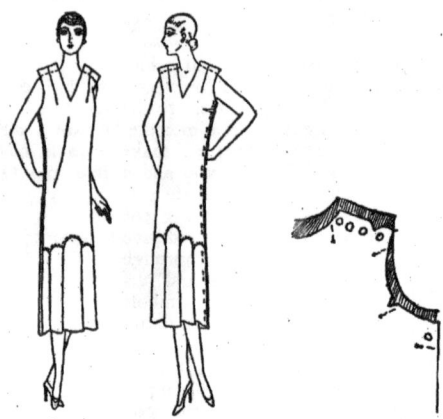

38. Wrinkles of this kind are easily removed

39. The back will need recutting the first time

A bust large in proportion to the rest of the figure will cause a garment to stand out at the center front and to draw in wrinkles running from the bust downward toward the underarm seam.

To correct this, rip the underarm seam up to within two inches of the armhole. Take up a dart at the underarm edge of the front at the bust line. Make the dart just deep enough so that the front hangs in a straight line below the bust. This applies to a frock with a shoulder dart. (Ill. 38.)

If the garment has a dart at bust line already, make a second dart instead of deepening the existing one, basting one just above and the other just below the fullest part of the bust. If the garment already has two darts, take in both equally.

The amount taken up in the dart must be taken from the length of the back. In a straight, one-piece garment, repin the underarm seam, so that the excess length comes at the lower edge and cut it off.

In a garment so constructed that the excess cannot be disposed of in this way, rip the back from the front, lay the pattern on the back, as in illustration 39, and recut.

Something to remember

After you have done this with one garment, you can, with future garments, adjust the length of the back before cutting the material, by laying a plait of the required width across the back of the pattern in line with the dart.

FITTING THE FIGURE WITH A FLAT BUST

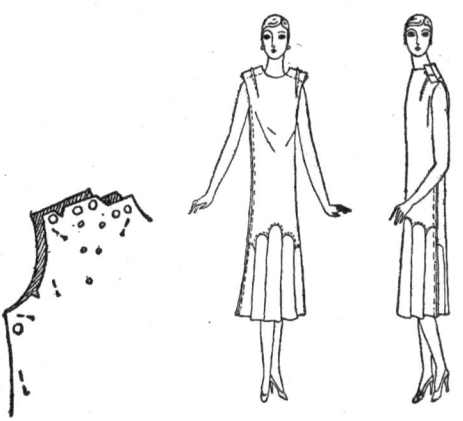

40. Recutting the shoulders and armholes

41. Fitting out wrinkles makes figure appear more normal

A figure that is flat at the bust causes wrinkles at the center front, through the bust, and makes the lower part of the garment appear to hug in.

If there is a dart in the shoulder, let it out as much as necessary to allow the garment to fall straight below the bust, making the alteration on the armhole side so that there is no change in the direction in which the dart runs. Repin the shoulder seam, lifting the shoulder edge of the front at the armhole enough to take out the wrinkle. Let the extra length in the shoulder edge of the front come at the armhole. Then lay the pattern on the front as shown in illustration 40 and recut the shoulder and armholes.

To adjust a garment with an underarm dart, rip the side seam and let out the dart as much as necessary. In a straight, one-piece dress of plain material, the excess length in front may be cut from the lower edge.

Where the construction of the garment makes this inadvisable, or in a garment made of plaids or crosswise stripes which should match at the seam, the excess should be taken from the top. Pin the front up on the shoulder as much as the dart was let out. After finding out just how much needs to be taken off lay the front of the garment down flat, place the pattern on it matching the notches at the underarm seam and recut.

The pattern has the final word

FITTING THE FIGURE WITH SLOPING SHOULDERS

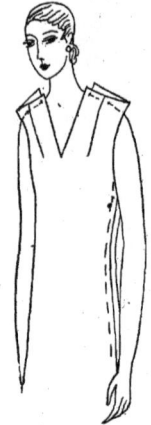

Wrinkles due to sloping shoulders removed by careful fitting

42. Before fitting

43. After fitting

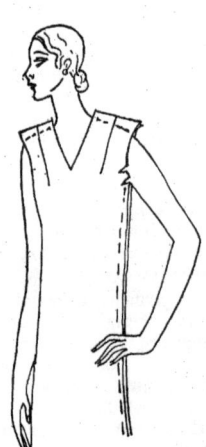

44. Alteration when slope is pronounced

If the garment is made with an open neck and the wrinkle is slight, the let-out seam provided at the shoulder of Butterick patterns will take care of the adjustment. Let this out at the neck until the wrinkles disappear, tapering the alteration to the regular line at the armhole.

If the garment has a high neck, or if the wrinkle is very pronounced, take up the shoulder seams at the armhole end of the seam as much as necessary, tapering the alteration off to nothing at the neck. This will decrease the size of the armholes and make them bind. Snip them—only slightly—at intervals under the arm until they feel perfectly comfortable.

FITTING THE FIGURE WITH SQUARE SHOULDERS

45. Before fitting

46. After fitting

Wrinkles due to square shoulders and their correction

If the wrinkle caused by square shoulders is very slight, the let-out seam on the shoulder will take care of the adjustment. Let this out at the armhole until the wrinkle disappears, tapering the alteration to nothing at the neck. This increases the size of the armhole, so the sleeve must be let out to fit.

If the wrinkle is pronounced, take up the shoulder seam at the neck, as much as necessary to remove the wrinkle, letting the adjustment slope to nothing at the armholes.

If the garment is to have a high neck, taking up the shoulder seams will make the neck too tight. Snip the neck edge a little at intervals until it feels comfortable, and trim it out.

47. Fitting the very bad case

FITTING THE FIGURE WITH ROUND SHOULDERS

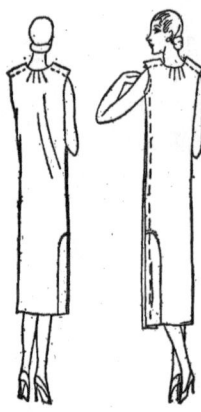

48. This wrinkle should be a danger signal to you

The penalty for bad posture

Round shoulders will cause the garment to hang in wrinkles from shoulderblades to underarm seams, and to draw across the back. Rip the underarm and shoulder seams and take up the shoulder edge of the back at the armhole, enough to make the back hang straight. The amount taken up should be tapered off to nothing at the neck. Ease the shoulder edge of the back to the front as much as you can without having it show. Repin the underarm seam with the side edge of the back as much higher than the side edge of the front, at the armhole, as the shoulder was raised, and trim off the excess from the back of the armhole. (Illustration 48).

When you bend over backwards

On an over-erect figure, the garment will show wrinkles at the upper part of the back, indicating too much length in the bodice. Take up the shoulder edge of the back at the neck, tapering it to nothing at the armhole. This will make the neck too high. Slash the neck edge at intervals until it feels comfortable. Take off the garment, baste the shoulder seam and trim off the neck edge on a line with the slashes. Try it on again before stitching the shoulder seams. (Ill. 49).

FITTING THE OVER ERECT FIGURE AND LARGE ARMS

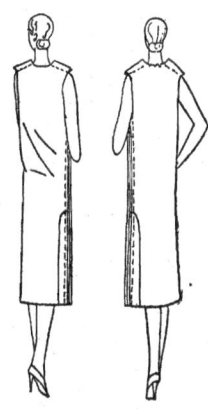

49. The too straight figure makes an unnecessary blousing in the back of the frock

If your arm is slightly larger than the average for your bust measure, the let-out seam which every Butterick pattern provides will take care of the adjustment. Let out this seam as much as necessary at the top, tapering the alteration according to the shape of your arm. The underarm seam of the garment must be let out the same amount at the armhole to take care of the added size in the sleeve. Taper the alterations gradually to nothing at the waistline.

For an arm that is very much larger than the average, the pattern should be adjusted before the material is cut, as described on page 23.

Arms should be in scale with the woman

If your sleeve has any tendency to span the arm be sure to let out the seam; otherwise it will be apt to break at the seam or elbow.

50. Using the convenient let-out seam

FITTING THE FIGURE OF PROMINENT ABDOMEN

52. Alteration to hide prominent abdomen

51. That unmistakable bulge   A prominent abdomen will make a frock stand out at the front. This is remedied in different ways for garments varied in cut.

For a one-piece garment with no dart across the hip, rip the underarm seam from the bottom up to the hipline (7 inches below the natural waistline) and take up a dart at the underarm edge of the front large enough to make the garment hang straight below the abdomen.

Taper this dart off gradually to nothing at the side of the abdomen. Rebaste the seam and try on the garment again to be sure it is all right. This will make the back longer than the front, but this can be taken off at the bottom. The dart can be covered with trimming.

If the one-piece garment already has a dart across the hip, rip the underarm seam and make the dart enough deeper at the underarm edge of the front to make the garment hang straight below the abdomen. Take this extra amount in on the lower side of the dart in order to keep the line of the dart the same as it was originally.

Something to remember about darts   After you have tried this on one garment and found out just the amount necessary to take up in the dart, you can, the next time, before cutting your material, take

FITTING RULES VARY WITH THE TYPE OF GARMENT

the length out of the back by laying a plait across the pattern of the back in line with the dart.

For a prominent abdomen in a garment with attached skirt, if the skirt is attached at about the hipline, take up a tuck or plait at the underarm seam just above the seam that joins the skirt to the body. This plait should be deep enough to make the garment hang straight from the abdomen to the bottom. It should be pinned all the way across the back and should taper from the underarm seam to nothing at the side of the abdomen. When the garment hangs just right, take it off and baste the skirt as much higher than it was as the amount pinned up in the plait, but do not cut this amount off until you have tried it on again to make sure that it hangs just right with the seam in a good line around the body. If the skirt is attached at or near the knees, the alteration should be made in the same way as for a one-piece dress.

Look at the sketches opposite for this

Altering waistbands; sometimes a skirt to be worn with a tuck-in blouse needs to be made a little tighter or looser at the waist.

If the waist is too large, stitch the seams a trifle wider than the pattern allowance, or, if there are darts, deepen them a little.

If the waist is too small, let it out at the darts or at the let-out seams.

In taking in the seams let the alteration slope gradually to the hip. In letting out the seams, the alteration should of course, run down to the bottom of the skirt.

For the wasp waist . . . . . and others

In a circular garment with one or more darts, the waist size can be made smaller or larger by taking in or letting out the darts. In a circular garment without darts, if only a small reduction is required, it may often be eased into the belt.

If the waist needs to be made very much smaller, it may be necessary to make a small dart at each hip.

If the waistline needs to be made larger, it can be done by raising the garment a trifle on the belt all the way around. A very little will increase the waist size a good deal.

If a plaited garment is too large or too small at the waist, the plaits should be made either deeper or shallower to fit the belt line.

Plaits are very easily adjusted

MAKING SMART CLOTHES
FINESSE IN FINISHING

That elusive French touch

One way in which the smart French or American custommade dress laughs the amateur version or the cheap manufactured copy to shame is in the details of finishing. Finishing done by hand or machine stitching should never show at all. Final touches should always have that light fresh appearance of having been accomplished with utmost dexterity and no seams must be anything but flat and almost unnoticeable.

The inside of a French dress reveals many interesting things. In the very best of them you find, usually, that one seam has been stitched on the machine for firmness, and then pressed absolutely flat (pressing of seams on every possible excuse is of the utmost importance in the final effect) and the seams finished with the utmost casualness. Either they are whipped, in an offhand way, or, if you choose to be a bit fancy, they are cut zigzag and then whipped so that ravelling is impossible. A good dressmaker always adores the selvedge, using it where it will show conspicuously if it is decorative, introducing it as a finish underneath, wherever possible.

Hems must be hand finished

Hems, if any, are never, never sewed by machine. The edges may have a fine bias tape stitched to them (not bound—this is just a little bunchy) but the tape is then sewed to the dress carefully by hand. If the hem or the neckline is finished by simple binding, this should be sewed firmly and the second seam, which is likely to show, should be done by hand in your finest stitches. Flaring skirts of wool sometimes have narrow hems that may be stitched decoratively several times. If you use lingerie touches, have them of the very finest, and sew them in as carefully after each washing as if you were making the dress for the first time. The whole effect may be ruined by a ruffly collar that has been hastily stitched in so that the thread shows, or misses connections at the place where it should meet effortlessly.

Those troubling lingerie straps

And, if you want a perfect effect, don't forget the invaluable little French trick of having a tiny strip inside the dress at the shoulder, one end of which snaps down and holds your lingerie straps in place. Nothing in the world looks more unattractive, no matter how exquisite the dress, than a woman constantly retrieving that piece of pink ribbon that keeps tumbling down over her shoulder.

THE DELTOR METHOD OF STEP BY STEP CONSTRUCTION

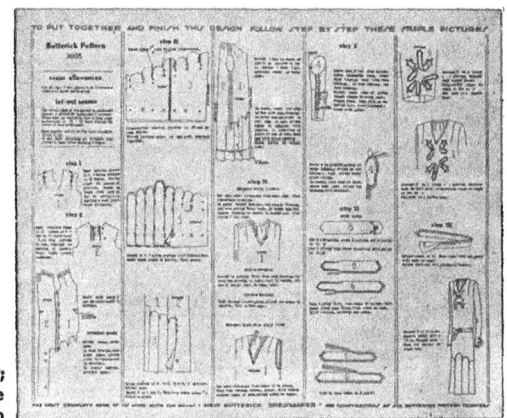

53. New Deltor; a complete working plan

The expert's way of working is always the most direct and quickest. The Deltor is the expert dressmaker's plan of working told in pictures. The beginner works with them with the same brilliant and unfailing success as the more experienced dressmaker who has a greater appreciation of their masterly directness. If you want to get the full value of your Deltor, you will, after you have used the layout side to adjust the length of the pattern and to cut your material, turn it over and follow the guidance of the illustrations and printed directions that make each step of the construction an easily understood operation and carry you on without delay or experiment from the first basting to the last adjusting of a belt or tie.

If you have never used a Deltor, read on and follow through the construction directions in this one. Each step in the construction of this frock has been carefully worked out by an expert dressmaker, accurately sketched and arranged in step-by-step order in vertical columns. See how clearly the pictures show how to crease on the line of small perforations and bring it over to the line of large perforations, to make the plaits in the front of the bodice; how to crease and stitch the tiny tucks at the neckline in the back.

A SPECIAL DELTOR FOR EVERY BUTTERICK DESIGN

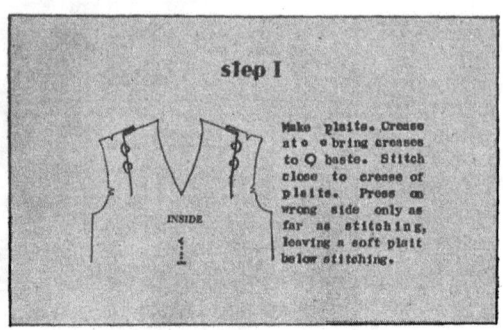

54. Clear cut illustrations and simple directions

This Deltor was made for the Butterick frock pattern which it illustrates, and every other Butterick pattern has a Deltor that has been made especially for that pattern. Each Deltor shows you the best way to cut, to put together and to finish every detail of the garment for which it was made, so that you can without experiment, which is a great consumer of time, make a garment that fits you well and that possesses all the distinction of line and finish that marks the work of the best couturiers.

Of course, you are now working in the material of which your garment is to be made, and instead of perforations you will have tailor's tacks; but you can see from the first illustration how simple a matter it is to follow the directions if you have made your tailor's tacks in one color for the small perforations and in another color for the large ones. With the Deltor illustration before you, you simply could not make the plaits run in the wrong direction.

Steps one and two, the Deltor says, ought to be taken before you stitch the parts of the garment together. The seams of the bodice are to be stitched and pressed open and you see that there are two ways of finishing the seams—one for wash fabrics and the other for silks and woolens.

It is wise to follow these sewing directions implicitly for so much depends on the care with which you make these first construction steps. Every Deltor includes complete directions for putting the garment together in every fabric suggested on your pattern envelope.

DRESSMAKING AS DRESSMAKERS DO IT

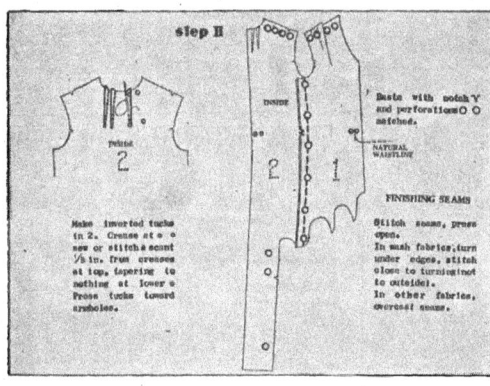

55. Each piece of pattern is shown clearly on the Deltor

With step three the flounce is put together, the plaits are laid, and the flounce is fastened to the bodice. Here again you will realize the value of the tailor's tacks with which you marked the locations of the perforations, for they help you not only in the basting and stitching of the seams, but also in the outside stitching. This stitching, you note, is to run down as far as the second perforation from the top.

The way to finish the hem is not overlooked by this helpful Deltor, which tells you the method that will give the best results if you are working with a woolen material, and another method for other fabrics.

In this case, if your frock is of wool the Deltor says to cover the raw edge of your hem with seam binding. If, however, it is of flat crepe or similar light weight fabric, the Deltor recommends that you turn in the raw edge of your hem, stitch close to the turning, clip the joining in the underfold of plait at top of hem and hold hem with blind hemming. In every case your Deltor tells you exactly how many inches of hem to turn up to achieve the fashion-right length. This length, of course, depends somewhat on your own individual height. You should check the finished back length of your garment which is always given on the back of the pattern envelope with the finished back length of a frock from your wardrobe that is the becoming length for you, and vary the depth of your hem accordingly.

YOU CAN BE AN EXPERT BEGINNING WITH ANY FROCK

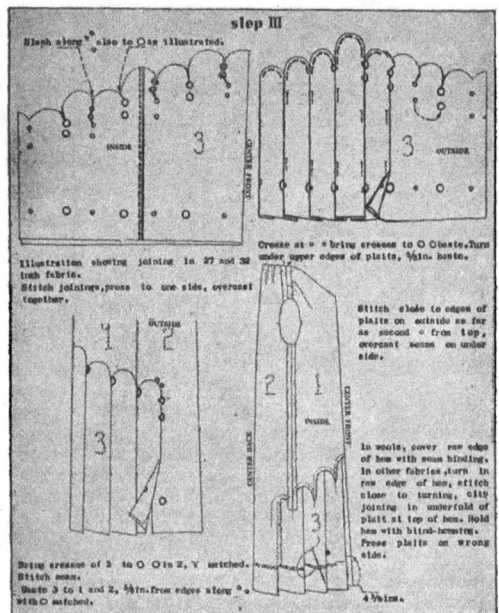

56. The Deltor simplifies such intricacies for you

It is often in seemingly unimportant details of this sort that a garment just fails to strike twelve, but there is no danger of falling short in the smallest point of perfection if you will let the Deltor help you from step to step as you make your garment.

Whether it is a filmy evening frock or a heavy winter coat with a fur collar that you are making, the Deltor that was made especially for your garment, and for no other, will make the process of construction a pleasure and the finished garment one that you can wear with all the satisfaction that results when a frock or coat is marked by the good lines and expert workmanship that characterize the creations of a couturier of the first rank.

There will be none of that slinking around corners that so often brands the unhappy author of a less than perfect creation and no embarrassing moments.

BINDING A NECK SMOOTHLY
AN ART YOU CAN ATTAIN

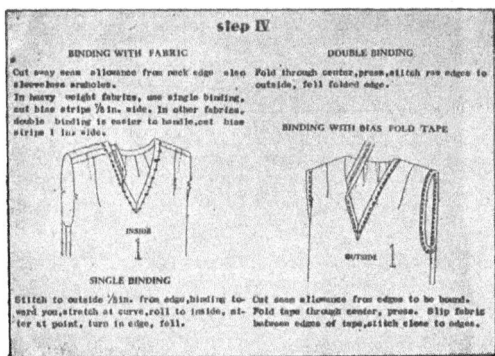

57. Fashion-right methods of finishing always shown

With step four you see how to finish the neck edge, and the armhole if you are making a sleeveless version of the frock. Here again the best methods are described for use with heavy fabrics and with light weight materials, and the details of making both single and double bindings are given for the benefit of inexperienced seamstresses.

Step five carries you on to the making of the sleeve. Some people find sleeve making troublesome, but it is hard to see how anyone could have trouble with this sleeve after looking at the illustration, with its let-out seam plainly marked by perforations, for which you have, of course, substituted tailor's tacks, and the little place at the elbow where the gatherings are put in, to give the ease that makes the sleeve comfortable without interfering with its good lines.

One of those nice little touches that give a perfect finish to a garment and that are often overlooked by inexperienced dressmakers is described in connection with the putting in of the sleeve. In wools, the Deltor says, the seam that holds the sleeve to the bodice ought to be clipped at the darts and pressed open across the top. This is the method of finish that gives that smooth even curve found in expertly tailored coats. The pressing, of course, is best done over a tailor's cushion which is illustrated and described on page 109 of this book.

DRESSMAKER DETAILS ARE GIVEN THEIR DUE

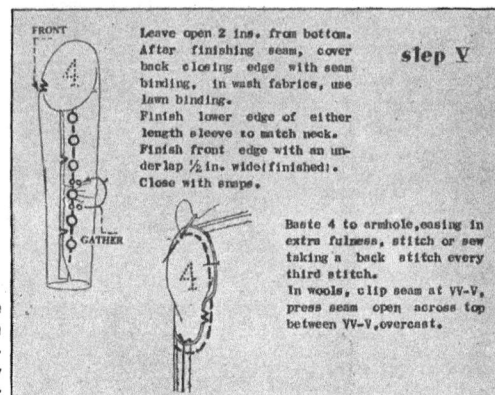

58. Put the sleeves in professionally—follow the Deltor

Step six makes clear every detail of the smart little bow effects that decorate the front of the bodice and the sleeves. These are cut following two of the pattern pieces, and the directions are perfectly clear: you cut eight strips like one pattern piece and four like the other, and you shorten half of each group by cutting them off at the line marked by perforations on the pattern and by tailor's tacks on your material.

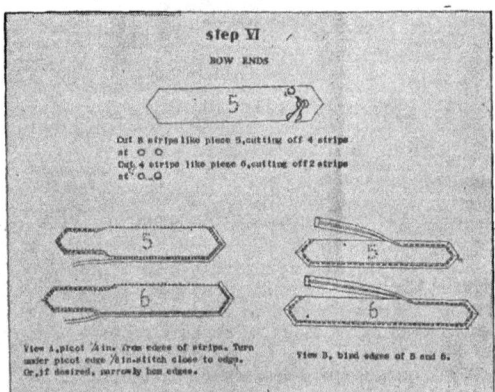

59. Little details that must be done expertly

THE FINISHING TOUCHES MADE DOUBLY EASY

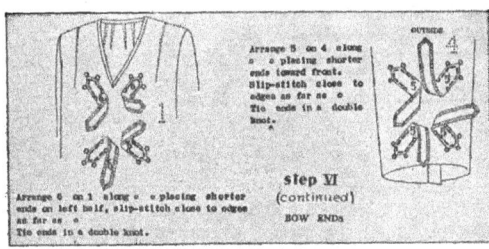

60. Placing and tacking tabs and bows and all the fripperies

As for the placing of these little bow effects, with the help of your tailor's tacks and the pictures in the Deltor you can pin them to position in a moment, and if you have been accurate in folding and cutting your material and in making your tailor's tacks there will be nothing more to do but sew them on and tie them together in a careless knot.

The last step is the making and attaching of the belt, which has been worked out for your convenience even to the eyelet for the buckle and the French tacks that hold the belt securely in place.

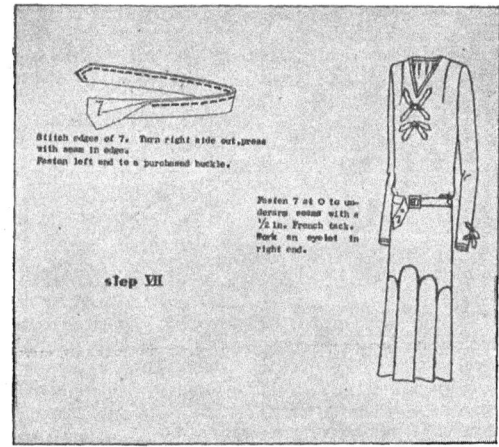

61. The waistline question settled for every frock

"SIT ON A CUSHION AND SEW A FINE SEAM"

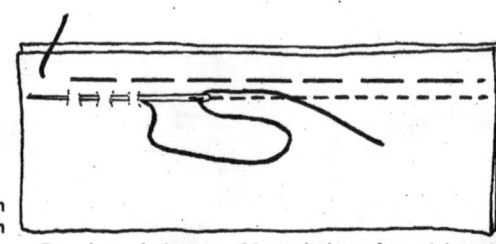

62. The even running stitch

Running stitches are short stitches of equal length, used principally for hand sewed seams on thin material where there is no great strain. They may be used in any other place where stitches of this kind are desired, such as hand run tucks and cordings used as trimming.

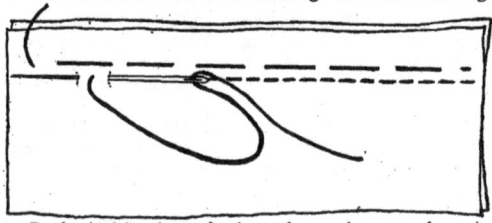

63. The firm backstitch

Backstitching is used where the sewing must be quite firm. Take a short stitch back on the upper side and a longer one forward on the under side. Each time you carry the needle back, insert it in the place in which it came up at the previous stitch.

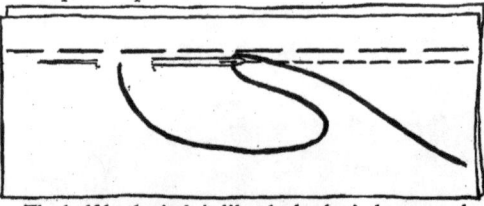

64. The half backstitch

The half backstitch is like the backstitch except that the needle is carried only half way back each time, leaving small spaces between stitches on the upper side. It is a firmer stitch than the running stitch but less firm than backstitching, which has almost the strength of machine stitching when carefully done.

SMOOTH SEAMS ARE AN INVESTMENT IN STYLE

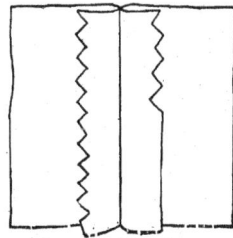

Good seams make a frock hang smoothly. In seaming garments, keep the cloth smooth, make the stitching perfectly even, and press carefully. The fabric and style of a dress govern the type of seam necessary, and the Deltor tells you which to use.

65. Pinking a plain seam

The simplest form of seam is the plain seam, made by laying the edges together and sewing in a straight line on the wrong side. In a closely woven material that does not fray easily, the edges may be simply notched or pinked and pressed open. On materials that ravel easily and that are too bulky to make into French seams, the edges may be overcast or bound.

For a French seam; baste the edges together on the right side of the garment

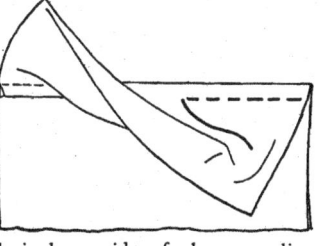

66. French seam; the double seam

and sew one-fourth inch outside of the seam line indicated by the pattern. Trim off edge to $\frac{1}{8}''$ and turn the garment wrong side out. Sew along the seam line, being sure to cover the raw edges. (Ill. 66) A variation of the French seam is the turned-in seam. Stitch a plain seam on the wrong side of the garment; turn the edges in toward each other, and hold with machine stitching, running stitches or overhanding.

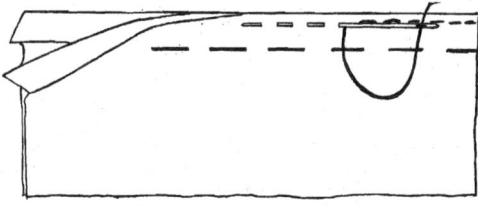

67. A turned-in French seam

KEEP THE EDGES OF YOUR SEAM WITHIN BOUNDS

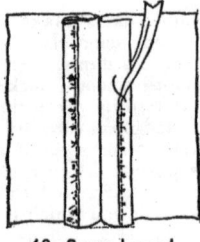

68. Seam bound with bias strips

Seams are often bound with bias strips. These may be bought already prepared, or can be cut from pieces of silk or sateen. For the binder attachment on your machine, cut and apply the bias strips as directed in the instruction book. If you are not using the attachment, cut the strips an inch wide and stitch one edge to the side of the seam, one-fourth inch in. Turn the binding over the edge and stitch inside the first stitching.

Straight seams may be bound with the ribbon known as seam binding. Fold this binding with one side a trifle narrower than the other, and press with a warm iron. Slip over the edge of the seam with the narrower side toward you, and run on by hand or stitch by machine, catching both edges with the one row of sewing.

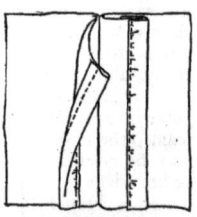

69. Seam bound with ribbon

A rolled seam is sometimes used in sheer materials. Baste the edges together, begin at the right end and roll tightly between the thumb and forefinger of the left hand. Whip the roll with stitches close together, making the stitches come under the roll and not through it. (Ill. 71.)

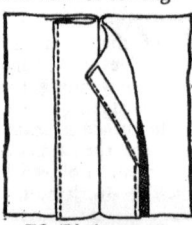

70. Plain seam, with turned edges

Plain seams may be finished simply by turning each edge under, away from the center, holding with running stitches.

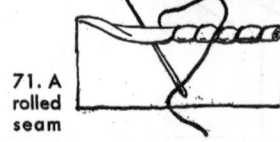

71. A rolled seam

EASY STITCHES THAT ARE ALWAYS USEFUL

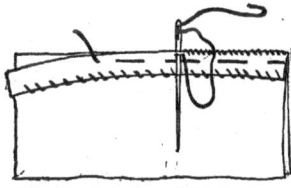

72. Overhanding folded edges

Overhanding is used to join folded edges or selvedges. Baste the edges together and sew with close stitches over and over, taking up only a few threads, so that the seam will open flat with no stitches showing on the right side.

Overcasting is a slanting stitch used to keep raw edges from raveling. In taking a stitch, point the needle toward your left shoulder; keep the spaces between the stitches even, and be sure that, before you start, the edges are trimmed off even.

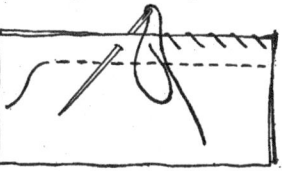

73. Overcasting seam edges

Catch-stitching is used to hold down seam edges. It is the preferred finish for flannel garments, because it makes a flat, soft seam. It may be used with both sides of the seam pressed in one direction, or the seam may be opened and each seam allowance catch-stitched.

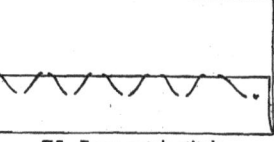

74. Catch stitching a flat seam

For a quick method of catch-stitching (Ill. 75): this stitch has not the strength of the first type and is used principally in millinery. It is used in dressmaking for a flat finish where the work is concealed.

75. Easy catch-stitching that hides the finish

YOUR SEWING MACHINE IS A FASHION ASSET

Take your machine out of the corner and give it a place in the sun

It may be taken as a matter of course that any one who does dressmaking has a sewing-machine, but many people own machines for years and never learn how much a sewing-machine can accomplish, the many almost unbelievable things it will do, and the real economy in its use.

Some people, too, get great quantities of work from their machines, but pay no attention to the quality—their seams are puckered or the thread is too tight on one side and too loose on the other—when the smallest turn of a screw would adjust the machine to the different materials and the sewing would be as good-looking as it is strong.

Whatever make of machine you own, the company which made it is the best authority regarding its care and operation. Their book of instruction will help you to become familiar with the machine itself, the places for oiling, the needed adjustments of needle, bobbin or tension screws, and especially with the various attachments used for so many fascinating methods of finishing and trimming garments and accessories.

KEEP YOUR MACHINE RUNNING ON HIGH

Among the attachments that come with most machines are binders, hemmers, rufflers and tuckers. The possibilities of these various attachments should be studied in the instruction book and practised until you can use them easily. They will save many hours of work and produce interesting effects.

With some machines it is possible to buy additional attachments, such as a small electric light that can be fastened to the arm of the machine, so that it throws light directly on the sewing and on the needle.

If you have bought a new machine, it is a good plan to read the instruction book from beginning to end before using it. Then take a few pieces of material, thread up the machine and experiment. Try it out not only on plain stitching but with all the attachments, making yourself familiar with their possibilities.

If there are any points that are not clear to you after you have read your book of instructions, ask for help from the personal instructor at the shop where you bought the machine; or, if you are not near enough for this, write to the manufacturer and explain your difficulty.

If you have had a machine for some time, but are not getting the best results, begin as though it were new. Sometimes just cleaning and oiling, tightening the belt, or readjusting the needles or tension will correct what seemed to be a serious difficulty.

Here are a few suggestions and facts in the use and care of your machine that you will find it worth while to keep in mind every day.

Sewing machines require daily oiling and cleaning if they are being used continuously. If used only a few hours a day, cleaning and oiling once or twice a week is enough. Always remove lint, dust, thread, etc., before oiling.

If you use bobbins, make sure that they are wound evenly and not too full. Avoid winding one color over another; the buried ends are likely to come out and cause trouble. Bobbins are inexpensive, and if you like to keep various colored threads wound and ready, it will pay you to have an adequate supply.

Regulate the length of stitch to suit the thread you are using and the material you are sewing. As a general rule, when stitching fine material, use a short stitch, a light tension, fine thread and a fine needle.

Treat your machine with great respect . . . . it pays

HOW LONG DO YOU WEAR YOUR SKIRTS

The lower edge line of a garment has much to do with its smartness. The correct length varies with the fashion and the wrong length can destroy the style effect. As in most fashions, there is usually an extreme as well as a conservative version of style length. It rests with the individual to choose what suits her taste and is becoming to her figure. In planning the length of a garment, it is best to allow about an inch for the give and take of making. For this reason and owing to differences in figures, it is necessary to turn the lower edge on the person who is to wear the garment. This should not be done until the sleeves are in and the rest of the garment all ready for finishing. The circular skirt, flounce or godet, being cut on the bias, will always stretch more or less. It stretches because its own weight draws it down. You should make it stretch before turning the lower edge so that it will not stretch after the edge is finished.

Baste the garment together and hang it up on a hanger, or on your dress form if it is not in use at the time, and let it hang for two or three days. At the end of that time, if the circular part of the garment extends only part way around, as in a godet, rip the seams that have bias edges while the garment is still hanging and let the bias edge drop as much as it will below the edge it was basted to. Do not pull but let it fall naturally; rebaste it to position. Then turn up the lower edge.

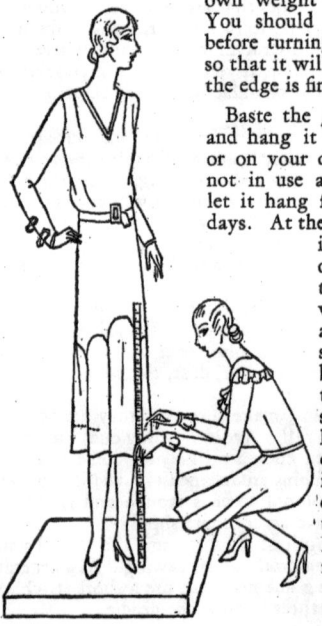

76. Marking position of the hemline

DO YOU EVER HANG YOUR OWN SKIRTS

To mark the lower edge, if you have someone to help you, paste a strip of paper around your yard stick the number of inches from the end that you wish your garment to come from the floor. If possible, stand on a skirt stand or table. The ruler can be moved around the skirt with the lower end resting on the stand or table on which you are standing, and pins inserted every two or three inches, in line with the mark you have placed on your yard stick.

If your garment is made with a circular front and straight back, it is wise to turn up the front three-eighths of an inch shorter than the back, so that if the front still stretches a little it will not appear longer than the back.

If you have no one to help you in hanging your skirt, stand along side of a table, the surface of which comes just below the hip. Standing against the edge of the table turn around slowly, putting pins into your garment every two inches, in line with the edge of the table.

This makes for easy dressmaking

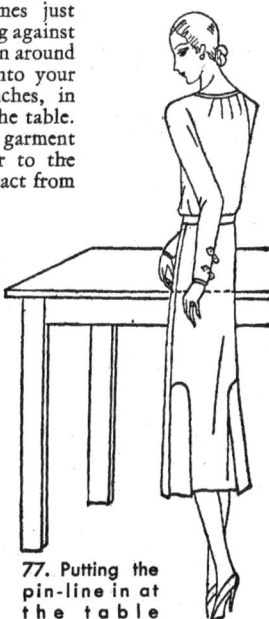

After removing the garment measure from the floor to the edge of the table; subtract from this measure the number of inches that you wish your garment from the floor. Lay your garment flat on a table and, with a yard stick measure down this number of inches from each of the pins and put in another pin-line.

For instance, if the table edge is 30" from the floor, and your finished garment is to be 12" from the floor, the second row of pins will be 18" below the first.

77. Putting the pin-line in at the table

EASY WAYS OF MAKING YOUR HEMS SMOOTH

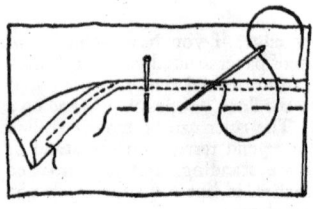

78. Hem suitable for straight or slightly gored skirts

A hem is made by turning the edge of the material over twice. The first turning should be narrow and must, of course, be perfectly even. The depth of the second turning depends on where the hem is used and the effect you want to give. The pattern gives you the correct depth for the design. To make the second turning the same depth throughout its length use as a marker a card notched the desired depth of the hem. If the hem is wide, baste it at both the top and bottom.

A hem for a slightly gored or straight skirt—the hem edge is turned under in the usual way. If an invisible sewing is desired, the turned-under edge of the hem is stitched close to the turning, but not to the garment, and then blindstitched neatly and carefully but not too tightly to the garment.

A straight hem can be finished with ribbon seam binding on silk or wool materials, and with bias-fold tape on heavy cottons or linen. Turn up the hem and stitch the edge of the seam binding to the upper edge of the hem without stitching through to the garment. Blindstitch the other edge of the seam binding to the garment.

A circular hem is often used on a garment that does not follow the grain of the material at the lower edge.

If the material is soft in texture, the top of the hem is simply turned under and a gathering thread run in

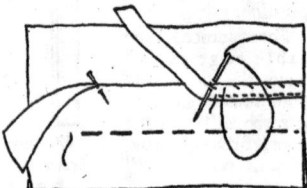

79. Seam binding makes a smooth hem finish

HEMMING CIRCULAR SKIRTS OF VARIOUS WEIGHTS

close to the turning. Draw the gathering thread till the top of the hem is the same size as the part to which it is to be sewed. Blind-stitch it or machine-stitch it to the garment.

If the material of the garment is of heavy weight, the upper edge should be gathered without turning it under and the raw edge should be covered with a strip of seam binding. The lower edge of this seam binding should be sewed to the hem but not to the garment.

Before sewing the top of the hem in place, slip a piece of muslin, cut the shape of the bottom of the garment, under the hem and press the hem flat, shrinking out as much of the fullness as possible. The piece of muslin will prevent the fullness in the hem from making marks on the garment during the pressing. The piece can be comparatively short and can be moved as the pressing is done.

After the hem has been pressed in this manner, hem the upper edge of the seam binding to the garment with invisible stitches.

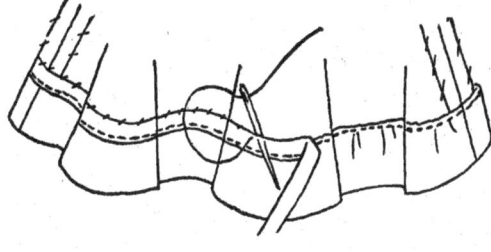

80. A circular hem finish suitable for heavy fabrics and tailored garments

In hemming, train the eye to keep the stitches even and true, take very small, almost invisible, stitches on the right side and stitches of an even length on the wrong side. Don't draw the thread tight, or leave it loose, and always use a fine needle and thread.

HEMMING STITCHES HAVE MUCH TO DO WITH STYLE

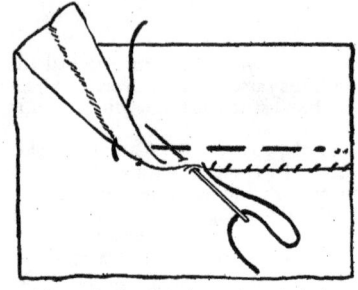

81. Slanting hemming stitch

To make the slant hemming stitch place the hem over the forefinger and under the middle finger of the left hand and hold it down with the thumb. Begin at the right hand and insert the needle through the fold, leaving a short end of the thread to be caught under the stitches.

Pointing the needle toward the left shoulder take a slanting stitch, taking up one or two threads of the material and the fold of the hem. At the end of the hem fasten the thread with two or three stitches.

If a new thread is needed start as at the beginning, tucking both the ends of the new and old threads under the fold of the hem, and securing them with stitches.

The straight hemming stitch is used where an edge is to be held close with stitches that should show as little as possible. Start it the same way as for slant hemming.

Insert the needle into the material as close as possible, to where you brought the thread through, bringing the needle up in a slanting position under the hem and out through the fold of the hem close to the edge. This stitch is preferred by tailors for felling linings in coats, etc., for the stitches show so little.

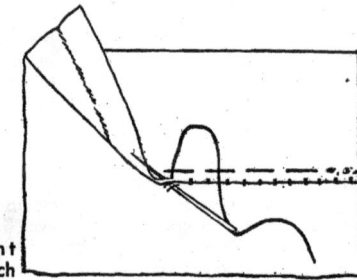

82. Straight hemming stitch

EACH STITCH HAS A METHOD OF ITS OWN

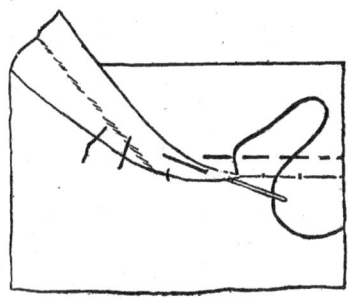

83. Making the slip stitch

Slip-stitching is used when it is necessary to have sewing that is invisible on both sides. It is not a strong sewing, but it is one of the most valuable stitches for finishing work in silk or wool. In this stitch it is necessary to take up only part of one thread in the material. This is what makes it invisible on the right side. Let the needle slip through the underside of the fold and bring it out through the crease so that the thread does not show on the fold, thus making it invisible on the wrong side.

Blind hemming is used when it is necessary to have the sewing invisible on the right side only. It is done more quickly than slip-stitching and is just as invisible on the right side of the garment. Take up only part of one thread in the material and insert the needle in the fold of the hem, using a rather long slanting stitch on the wrong side. It is not a strong sewing but in many cases is used for hems or facings on silk and wool as it makes the impression of the hem invisible from the right side.

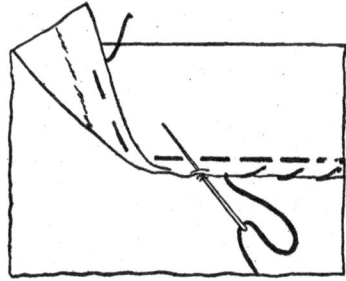

84. Making blind hemming stitches

TRUE BIAS GUARANTEES SMOOTHNESS IN FINISHING

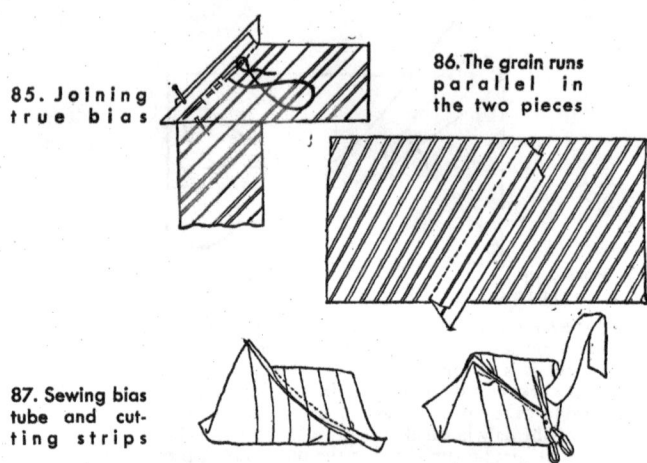

85. Joining true bias

86. The grain runs parallel in the two pieces

87. Sewing bias tube and cutting strips

Bias strips are useful not only for binding seams but for all sorts of trimmings and edgings. They may be bought in various designs and fabrics, or they may be cut from the same material as the garment. The way to find a true bias is described on page 31. When you have marked your line, as suggested there, measure from it and mark as many lines as you need, being sure that each line is equally distant from the last, throughout its length.

To join bias strips, lay the ends together as illustrated and baste or stitch in a seam. When the joined ends are opened out, the grain of both pieces runs in the same direction.

If bias strips have to be made from small pieces, there is a short cut that will save time and do away with the necessity of much piecing together. Trim your material to a straight grain on all four sides. Find the true bias, mark as many strips as can be cut from the piece, and cut off the triangular piece at one corner. Then pin two opposite edges together, leaving the beginning of the binding free, and matching the other marks carefully, as shown in illustration 85. Stitch the seam and begin to cut at the free end, following the line around and around the tube, as in illustration 87.

PRACTICAL HINTS ON ATTRACTIVE NECKLINES

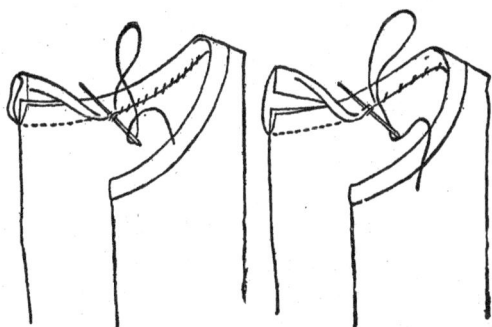

88. Double binding for light fabrics and lingerie

89. Single binding for the heavier fabrics and edges

Bias bindings may be single or double. In wools, heavy cottons or linens use a single binding, as a double binding of these materials would be too bulky. Double binding is better in the lighter weight materials, because it is easier to handle.

In using any bias binding be careful not to let it twist or pull crooked.

For a double binding, cut bias strips of the material a trifle more than four times as wide as you want the finished binding to be, plus an allowance for a seam on each edge. Join the strips, if necessary, and press the seams open. Fold the finished strip through the center and press. Stitch the raw edges to the outside of the edge that is to be bound, the seam's width from the edge, with the binding toward you. Roll to the inside and sew the folded edge to the line of sewing that holds the outside.

For a single binding, cut bias strips twice the width of the finished binding, plus allowance for a seam on each edge. Stitch one edge to the outside, the seam's width from the edge, with the binding toward you. Roll to the inside. Turn in the edge the width of the seam allowance and sew it to the line of stitching that holds the outside.

A CURVED EDGE IS REALLY EASY

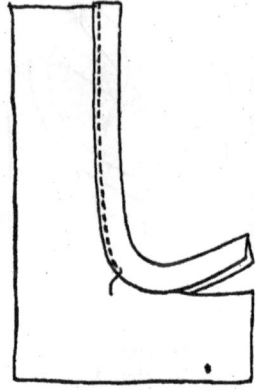

90. Slip fold of binding over edge

Any straight edge can be bound with braid or ribbon, and a curved edge can be bound with a braid that will stretch. To bind with braid or ribbon, fold through the center and press. Slip the material between the edges of the binding, baste and stitch, or put it on with the binding attachment of your machine. Dampening braid at the ends makes it easier to handle.

There are two ways of binding with bias-fold tape. The first is to stitch one edge of the tape to the outside along the crease in the tape, with the tape toward you, roll to the inside and sew the folded edges to the stitches that hold the outside. The second method is to fold it through the center, slip it over the edge that is to be bound, and sew through both sides with one row of stitching.

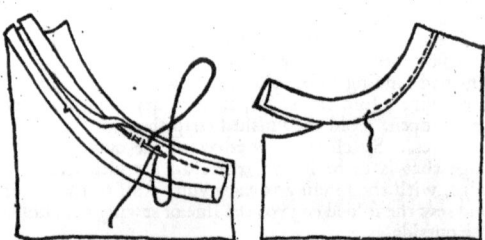

91. Applying bias-fold tape

A scalloped edge, especially in a sheer material, is charming bound with a bias strip. The work must, of course, be done carefully so that the binding is smooth and even and that every little miter is put in sharp and true.

AND SCALLOPS ARE NOT ALARMING

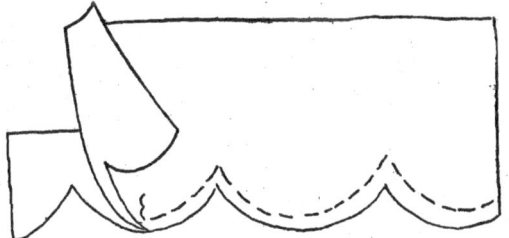

92. First step

Mark the outline of the pattern on tissue-paper about two inches wider than the deepest part of the scallops, and baste the scalloped edge of the material to the outline on the tissue-paper.

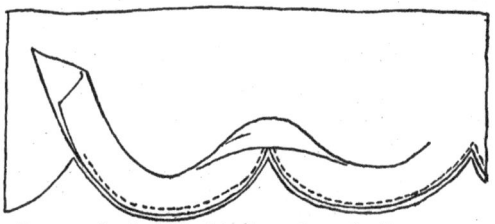

93. Second step

Baste and stitch the binding, through the paper, to the edge that is to be bound, with the binding toward you, stretching it at the points of the scallops as shown in the illustration.

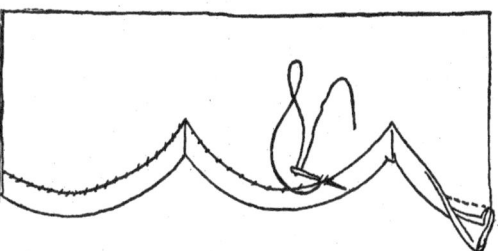

94. Third step in binding scalloped edge

Tear the paper away from the edge, roll the binding to the inside, lay the fullness at each point in a tiny plait or miter and sew the folded edge to the line of stitches holding the binding to the scallops.

FACING FACTS THAT ARE OF USE TO YOU

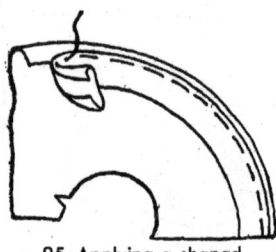

95. Applying a shaped facing at edge of collar

A facing is often used for the finish of an edge. A frock can sometimes be remodeled by using a facing instead of a hem at the bottom of the skirt. A hem, however, is better than a facing for transparent materials, as the joining seam shows through and does not look well unless the edge is trimmed in some manner that conceals the seam. Facings may be sewed to an edge and then turned, or the edge may be turned first and the facing applied.

A straight facing may be used if the edge to be faced is a perfectly straight line. The facing may be cut lengthwise or crosswise of the material.

A bias facing is used if the edge to be faced is slightly curved, for the bias facing can be stretched to fit the shape of the edge. Press the facing, stretching it at the outer edge and shrinking the inner edge as you do so.

A shaped facing (illustration 95) is cut the same shape and on the same grain of the material as the part to be faced. It may be used on all edges which are curved or irregular.

Ribbon seam binding is sometimes used for facing. Turn under the edge to be finished. If it is curved, clip it to make it lie flat. Sew the seam binding with a running stitch, easing the straight edge of the ribbon if it is being sewed to a curve. Tack the inner edge invisibly.

When facing a slashed opening, do not slash until the facing is on. Cut and baste the facing to the garment following instructions given in your Deltor. Taper the sewing from 3/8 inch each side of the center

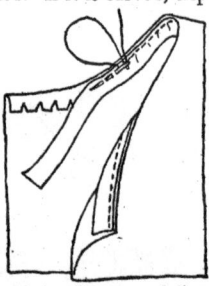

96. Another use of ribbon seam binding

SLASHES AND CURVES MAKE SPECIAL FACING DEMANDS

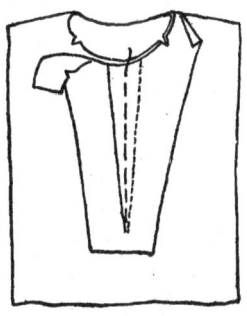

97. Sew facing to right side of frock

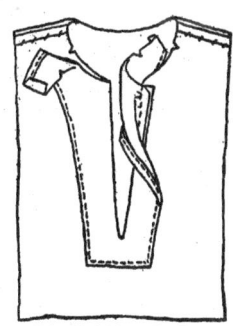

98. Finishing facing on a slashed opening

at the neck to ⅛ inch in order to have the lower end of the opening as nearly a point as possible. To keep the stitching in a straight line, draw a line with tailor's chalk and a ruler and stitch on the chalk line. Cut through the center almost to the lower end of the stitching. Turn the facing to the wrong side and baste. Turn in the loose edge of the facing and stitch close to the turning but not to the garment.

A corded facing makes an attractive-looking and firm finish for neck edges and the bottoms of sleeves. Cut a bias strip an inch and a quarter wide and sew one end to the end of a fine cord, placing the cord a little nearer one edge than the other. Fold the strip lengthwise over the cord and hold it in with running stitches placed as close as possible to, but not through, the cord which should run free in the casing so that it can be pulled up to fit curved edges.

Baste facing flat to edge and slip-stitch in place.

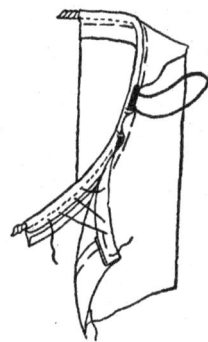

99. Slipstitching cord into place at neck

FIRM BUTTONHOLES GIVE GOOD SERVICE

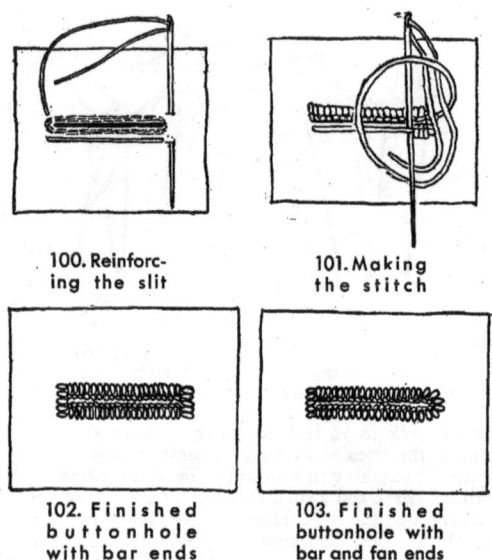

100. Reinforcing the slit

101. Making the stitch

102. Finished buttonhole with bar ends

103. Finished buttonhole with bar and fan ends

A well-made garment that is otherwise perfect may be greatly injured in appearance by badly made buttonholes. They should always be marked before they are cut. When making a row of buttonholes, mark the position for the two ends of the row and divide the distance between into the desired number of spaces. Cut the slit on the thread of the goods, if possible, and make it large enough to allow the button to slip through easily, as a properly made buttonhole becomes tighter after it is worked.

With the buttonhole scissors carefully test the length for the slit and make a clean cut with one movement of the scissors. One of the most noticeable faults in buttonholing results from an uneven or ragged slit. This may be caused by dull scissors or by the slipping of the fabric. To prevent the material from slipping, baste, or run several rows of machine stitching around the mark before cutting. The machine stitching gives a very firm edge to the finished buttonhole and is especially good for loosely woven materials that may ravel.

THE POSITION OF THE BUTTONHOLE IS EVERYTHING

If the buttonhole is in an upright position, as in the center of a plait, or in any other case where the strain does not come at the ends, the buttonhole with a bar at both ends is used. If the strain on the buttonhole comes at one end so that the button requires a resting-place, as in a cuff or belt, use the buttonhole with the round end.

<small>Consider the location</small>

Buttonholes are strengthened with strands of thread to prevent the edges from stretching. Bring the needle up at one end and, allowing the thread to lie along the edge of the cut on the right side of the material, make a small stitch under the material at the other end. Do the same on the other side of the cut as shown in ill. 100 on the opposite page.

When working a buttonhole in a coat where interlining is used and there is danger of the material slipping so the interlining will show, the edges may be overcast before the buttonholes are worked. To make the stitch, place the buttonhole over the forefinger of the left hand, holding it in position with the thumb and second finger. Begin to work the buttonhole close to the corner or starting-point. Insert the needle and, while it is pointing toward you, bring the double thread as it hangs from the eye around to the left and under the needle. Draw the needle through the loop, letting the thread form a purl exactly on the edge of the slit. Continue these stitches to the opposite end, being careful to make them the same depth and close together.

If you are making a double barred buttonhole, when you have worked one side, pass the needle up and down through the goods until two or three threads cross the end of the slit quite close to the buttonhole-stitches. Turn the work around so that the bar end is toward you and make several buttonhole-stitches over the bar and through the material. Work the other side of the buttonhole and the second bar.

For a round-end buttonhole, when you come to the outer end, take the stitches on a slant, inserting the needle each time at a little different angle until the end is rounded. Continue the work on the other side. Finish the inner end with a bar.

A buttonhole, to have a really professional air, should have the stitches taken rather shallower than deep. The material and its fraying liabilities will govern the actual depth.

<small>Stitches deep enough but not too deep</small>

BOUND BUTTONHOLES ARE EASILY MADE

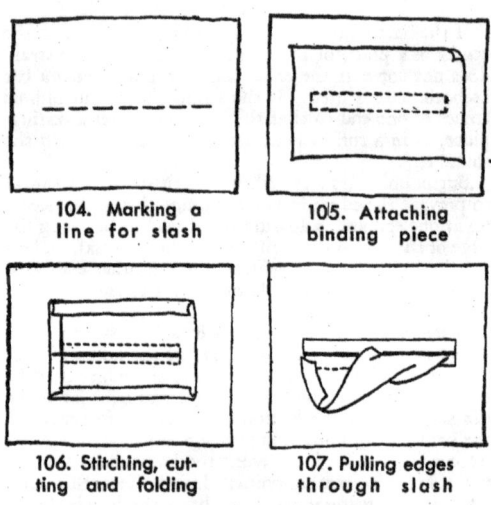

104. Marking a line for slash

105. Attaching binding piece

106. Stitching, cutting and folding

107. Pulling edges through slash

The bound buttonhole can be used on garments of wool, silk, linen, cotton or mixed materials. It gives a finished look to a coat or dress and is particularly effective when the binding is in a contrasting color, although binding is frequently of the same material as the garment.

There are two ways of binding a buttonhole. In either case, the position and length of the buttonhole should be marked on the garment with colored thread. When the wrong side of the buttonhole is to show, use for binding a bias strip of material 1⅝ inches wide and ¼ inch longer than the finished buttonhole. Baste the binding to the garment with its center lying along the buttonhole mark and right sides together. Stitch one-eighth of an inch from each side of the buttonhole mark and across the ends. (Illustration 105.)

Turn in the outer edges of the binding ⅛ of an inch and press. (Illustration 106.) Cut the buttonhole along the line marked by the basting (now covered by the stitched-on binding,) cutting through both garment and binding right up to the stitching, but not through it.

Push the binding through to the wrong side of the

FOLLOW THIS STEP
BY STEP METHOD

garment (Illustration 107.) and slip-stitch it to position along the sewing line of the outside. Slip-stitch the ends so they will not fray.

When the wrong side will not show, use for binding a bias strip 1¾ inches wide and ¾ of an inch longer than the finished buttonhole.

Baste and stitch the binding as before, and cut the buttonhole, cutting the corners diagonally to the stitching. (Illustration 108.)

Push the binding through to the wrong side of the garment, laying the fullness at the ends in a box plait. (Illustration 110.) Fasten the plaits with a few overhand stitches and sew the binding to position along the sewing line of the outside, but do not turn the edges under. Press well.

If the garment has a facing, baste it flat about an inch from the buttonhole. Cut a straight line in the lining at the buttonhole. Turn in the edges of the facing, and slip-stitch to the binding.

Either of these methods may be used in binding slashes for any purpose, such as a double opening through which a neck frill or belt is to be slipped. A finish of this sort, carefully made and thoroughly pressed, adds a note of expert tailoring to any garment.

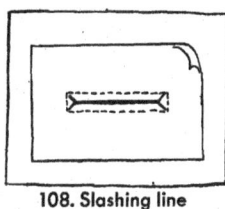

108. Slashing line for buttonhole

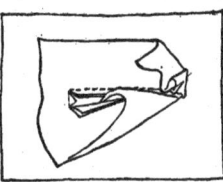

109. Pulling binding through slash

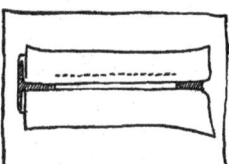

110. Folding the piece and fastening

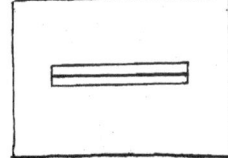

111. The finished bound button hole

PLACKETS BOUND OR FACED IMPROVE A FROCK

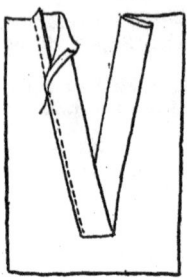

112. Continuous bound closing with no seam

Closings in sleeves and skirts for the tuck-in blouse mode require careful workmanship so that there shall be no bulging of the overlap. For a continuous lap closing, frequently used at the bottoms of sleeves, cut a strip twice the length of the opening and twice the width of the finished underlap plus ⅜ inch on each edge for a seam. When used as a slash, lay the lap along the edge of the opening with the right sides of lap together and sleeve together and stitch a narrow seam, running it to a point at the end of the opening. Turn the free edge under and hem it close to the sewing. The closing may be fastened with tiny snaps, or buttons may be sewed to the underlap and buttonholed loops worked on the edge of the overlap.

A flat placket should never gap, so use as many fastenings as the length requires. Be sure they are sewed behind the edge

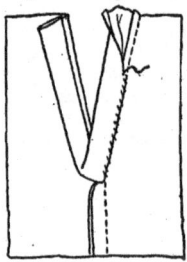

113. Continuous closing above seam, slashed

of the seam so that they won't show when the placket is fastened.

Today when more fitting on frocks makes more side placket closings necessary, it becomes part of good dressmaking to learn to make them quickly and professionally. Remember the bindings should be narrow, flat, smooth, secure and as invisible as possible from the right side.

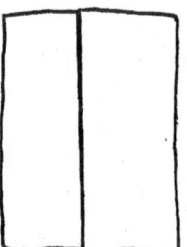

114. This closing is invisible on right side

SKIRTS HAVE THEIR OWN MEANS OF CLOSING SNUGLY

A closing in a skirt which is to be worn with a tuck-in blouse should be deep enough to slip easily over the shoulders. The design of the skirt regulates the position and finish of the placket. The closing may be fastened with snaps or with hooks and eyes or blind loops.

To make a placket at a seam, face with silk or other thin material the right side of the opening which is to serve as the overlap. Stitch from right side of hem to the wrong side or hem to the wrong side with invisible stitches. Sew an un-

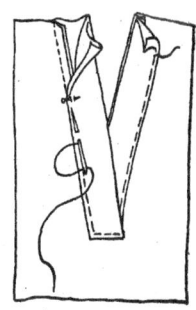

115. A faced and bound placket

derlap of material an inch and a half wide, finished, to under side of the opening and line this underlap with silk.

Illustration 115 shows a simple finish for a placket which may be used on a slash where no strain comes on the placket. The overlapping edge is finished with a facing and the under edge with an underlap. The facing can be machine-stitched

116. Inside of skirt placket

or finished invisibly by hand according to the finish of the skirt.

A placket is easily made at the under fold of a plait. Cut through the crease or under fold in the plait to the regular placket depth. Bind both cut edges with binding ribbon or thin silk. (Ill. 114.)

Where there is no strain on a placket, fastenings are needed only at the top.

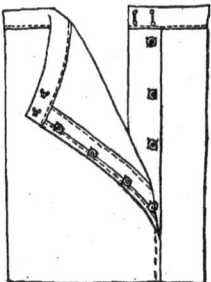

117. Tailored closing viewed from above

HEMSTITCHING BY MACHINE IS NOT FOR HEMS ALONE

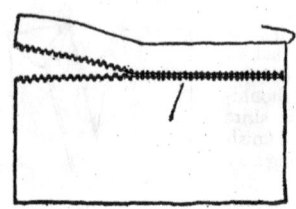

118. Picot edge; cut machine hemstitching

Machine hemstitching is used on blouses, dresses, lingerie, collars, and jabots, to put together seams, finish hems and put on trimmings. It is used also as a decoration, either in straight rows or in a fancy design. Prices for the work vary, but it is not expensive and any plaiting establishment or the salesroom of a sewing machine company will do it.

If the line which is to be hemstitched is irregular, so that it must be marked with bastings, be sure to use thread of the color in which the hemstitching is to be done, because it is impossible to pull out bastings that have been hemstitched. Where the stitching is to be in straight lines or along an edge, it may not be necessary to baste the line; a pin put in here and there to show the direction is usually all the machine operator requires.

For machine hemstitching keep the garment as nearly flat as possible. Seams that are not to be hemstitched should not be basted or sewed until after the hemstitching is done. If a cuff is to be hemstitched to a sleeve, for instance, leave the sleeve seam open until the hemstitching is done.

Seams on which machine hemstitching is used as a trimming or finish should be basted flat with both edges of the seam turned toward one side and pressed. An invisible seam for transparent materials can be made by machine hemstitching an ordinary seam on the wrong side and trimming off the edges. (Ill. 119.)

Picot edging is simply machine hemstitching cut through the center. (Ill. 118). It makes a dainty and yet strong finish for edges of collars, sleeves, flounces, etc.

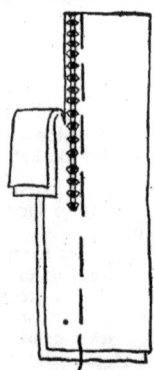

119. Machine hemstitching as a seam finish

HAND HEMSTITCHING FOR THOSE LINGERIE TOUCHES

A foundation for machine hemstitching may be necessary under bias edges and under thin materials. Some operators, however, have their machines adjusted to light work, and prefer not to have a foundation. It is advisable to find out before taking your material to the hemstitcher whether or not she wants the foundation used. In cases where foundations are required, mousseline de soie or very thin lawn may be used under georgette crêpe, chiffon, lace, etc.

The foundation for machine hemstitching done on the bias of the material can be a straight strip of the same material or one of the foundations mentioned above, one-half inch wide, basted underneath the line to be hemstitched. If no material for a foundation is at hand, baste the article to a piece of firm paper and stitch it by machine along the line for the hemstitching. This stitching keeps the edge from stretching and gives the operator the correct line for machine hemstitching. The paper should be torn away before the material is sent to the operator. Paper can also be used in this way under straight edges of thin material when you do not wish to use a foundation.

Hand hemstitching is a line of open-work made by drawing out parallel threads and fastening the cross threads in successive small clusters. It makes an attractive finish as a hem or may be used as a decoration for fine underwear, small children's frocks and lingerie collars and jabots. It may be used at the top of a hem or to hold a tuck, or it can be worked on a single thickness of material. It can, of course, be worked only in straight crosswise or lengthwise lines, which are often combined to make a corner.

The straight and narrow path for all hemstitching

Hemstitching may be done from left to right or from right to left, but many people find the first way the easier. When using it as a hem, insert the needle in the under fold of the hem at the left-hand edge. Hold the work over the forefinger of the left hand, keeping the thumb over the thread. Take up four or five threads with the needle, and draw the needle through, holding the sewing thread firmly by the left thumb. At the extreme right of the gathered threads take a short stitch in the fold of the hem, as shown in illustration 120, and draw the thread through. Now take up the same number of threads as before, and repeat.

For double hemstitching, draw the threads as for

HAND HEMSTITCHING GIVES AN EXQUISITE EFFECT

plain hemstitching and baste the hem in the same way. Work the first line as described for plain hemstitching, then turn your work so that the opposite side of the drawn threads is toward you. Make a second row of hemstitching in the same way, taking up the same groups of thread as before. (Illustration 121.) Take the little stitch between the groups through the edges

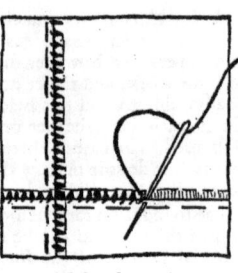

120. Single hemstitching

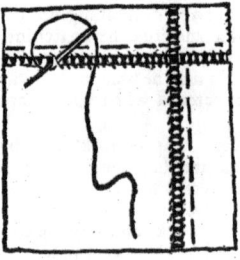

121. Double hemstitching

of the material instead of through the fold of the hem as in the first row.

Serpentine or fagot hemstitching is worked the same as double hemstitching except that in the second row of stitches half of the threads of one cluster and half of the threads of the next cluster are grouped together, giving a slanting or serpentine effect. (Illustration 122.)

For this type of hemstitching the groups must contain an even number of drawn threads so that they can be divided evenly. Otherwise the effect of the clusters will be irregular and uneven when finished, sacrificing the perfection of detail that is the charm of this type of hand work.

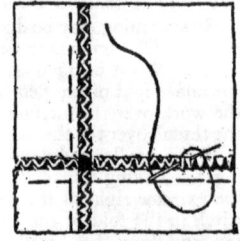

122. Fagot hemstitching

PLAITED FRILLS "PICOTED" FOR CUFFS AND COLLARS

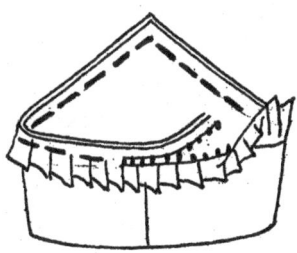

123. A secure finish for a plaited frill

This illustration from the Deltor shows you an easy way to make a plaited frill for cuffs and collars. Put a basting ⅜ of an inch from one edge of the fabric and other bastings 1⅝ inches apart. Use same color thread so it need not be removed. Machine hemstitch on every other basting, press on wrong side, cut through center for picot edge. (Illustration 124.)

Make as many strips as you need, keeping in mind that three yards of plain material make only about one yard of plaited edging. Join the strips with tiny French seams and send to be side plaited in ¼ inch plaits. Baste frill to your collar and cuffs, with raw edges even. Picot the seam, and turn the frill up. (Ill. 123.)

There is an interesting way of using picoting invisibly as a finish for fine materials where a very fine, yet firm edge is necessary. Have the edge hemstitched and cut through the stitches to make the picot, then turn the picot under and stitch it flat from the right side, close to the edge. This is an excellent finish for bottoms of circular flounces and tips of set-on panels.

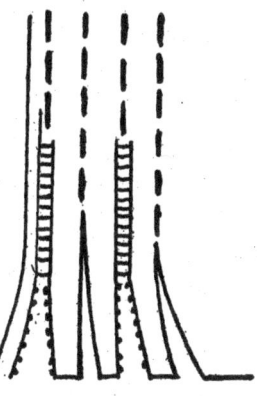

124. Preparing the strips for plaiting

HAND STITCHING FOR THAT FRENCH TOUCH

The fagot-stitch is a style of hand-made trimming that is always popular and attractive for yolks and collars, or for joining parts of a frock. Sometimes it is used in lingerie to hold a ribbon drawstring.

The design of the work should first be traced on a piece of stiff paper. Or, as in the case of a yoke or collar where a fitted shaping is required, a fitted pattern should be cut of stiff paper, and the ribbon, braid or folds of the material basted evenly in position. When the fagoting is to be applied to the garment in fancy design, and the material underneath

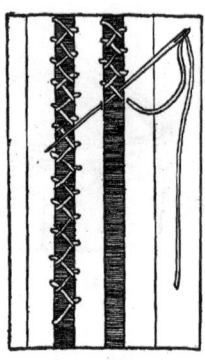

125. Fagoting makes a lacey insertion for your frocks

the stitches is to be cut away afterward, the entire piece of work should be smoothly basted over paper, and the line of spacing which represents the fagot-stitching outlined with chalk or basting cotton.

The simple fagot-stitch is done by crossing first from left to right, and recrossing from side to side between the folds of the material, taking a small stitch in the edge. The needle in crossing each time passes under the thread of the preceding stitch, thus giving the threads a slight twist at the edge. (Ill. 125).

There are many variations of fagoting and in any garment where this type of decoration is recommended, the Deltor shows how to work the stitches and how to apply them to the place where they are to be used.

Double overcasting is used to finish the edges of blouses, thin dresses and children's clothes. Turn under a hem one-eighth of an inch deep and baste it. Hold the work loosely in the left hand. Fasten the thread at the right and overcast toward the left. When the entire edge is overcast, overcast in the opposite direction, inserting the needle at the base of each stitch in the previous row. The stitches of the two rows will cross at the edge.

SIMPLE STITCHES CAN BE MOST DECORATIVE

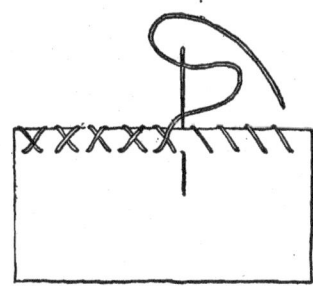

126. Double overcasting shows the cross

A variation of double overcasting is cross double overcasting. Make it as described on page 86, but in the second row put the needle half way between the stitches of the first row, bringing the crossing between the top and bottom of the hem instead of at the edge.

Blanket-stitch is used as a trimming on blouses and on children's dresses. It can be worked in any heavy thread, such as rope silk, embroidery cotton or linen, or wool.

Do not use a knot, but secure the thread by running one or two stitches toward the edge, holding the thread under the left thumb. Insert the needle the depth required, bringing it out under the edge.

Cross-stitch, French-knot embroidery, braiding, beading and embroidery are worked from transfer designs. New and fascinating designs for hand trimming will be found in your Butterick Quarterly. Every transfer gives illustrated directions for making the stitches suitable for that design.

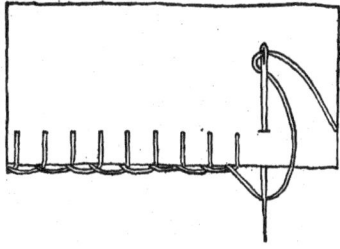

127. Blanket stitching is charming for children's clothes

FEATHERSTITCHING AND SMOCKING HAVE WON FAVOR

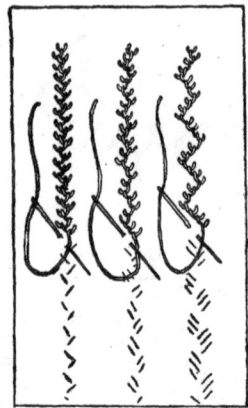

128. Variations of the useful featherstitch

Featherstitching never loses its popularity for small children's garments and fine lingerie. It may be used in circles or scrolls or straight lines, and is particularly attractive between rows of tiny hand run tucks.

Run a colored thread along the outline to mark the center line for the featherstitching. To make the single stitch, knot the thread and then bring the needle up through the material. Hold the thread down over the line with the left thumb. Insert the needle a little to the left of this line, and take a short, slanting stitch toward the right, drawing the needle out while the thread is held down smoothly by the left thumb. Then hold down the thread on the center line and take a stitch of equal length on the right side and draw it out as before.

For the double combination take two stitches to the left and two to the right each time before crossing the center line, and for the triple combination take three stitches. The beauty of featherstitching depends on its evenness. Marks on the illustration indicate the position and direction for the stitches.

Smocking is a style of trimming particularly suited to children's clothes, and much used on the better class of children's garments here and abroad. It is used for frocks, infants' coats and little boys' suits. It is effective in colors on dresses of fine white batiste, nainsook, plain lawn, handkerchief linen, cotton voile, very fine cotton crêpe and silk mull. It is also used on the heavier cotton materials in white or plain colors, on chambray, serge, broadcloth, crêpe de chine, etc.

Fullness for smocking is estimated by the pattern
It is very easy to do with the Butterick transfers, which not only give the design of the smocking but instructions for working it. Transfers recommended for various patterns have all been carefully tested.

FINE GATHERING HAS ITS REWARD

Gathering or shirring may be done either by hand or by machine. To gather by hand, make a row of small running stitches. The stitches may be the same length as the spaces, or the spaces may be twice the length of the stitches. Always begin by inserting the needle from the wrong side to conceal the knot. It is better to slip the stitches along on the needle and not remove it from the material.

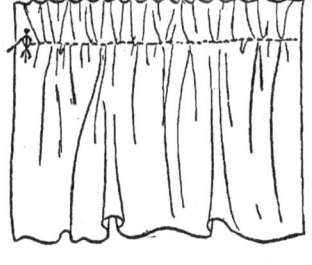

129. Simple gathering by hand

With a single row of gathering it is necessary to stroke the stitches in order to make them lie straight. When the gathering is completed, remove the needle and draw the gatherings up tight. Place a pin vertically, close to the last stitch, and wind the thread several times around the pin in the form of an 8. (Ill. 129.)

Hold the work between the thumb and fingers of the left hand, with the thumb below the gathering-thread. Put the side of the needle well above the gathering-thread and press the little plait under the thumb, drawing the needle down. (Ill. 130.)

Do not turn the point of the needle toward the material, as it scratches and weakens the material. Continue entirely across the gathers and stroke the material above the thread as well as below.

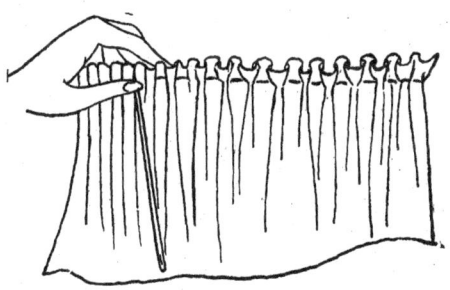

130. Stroke gathers to make them lie straight

DOUBLE AND TRIPLE ROWS KEEP THEMSELVES STRAIGHT

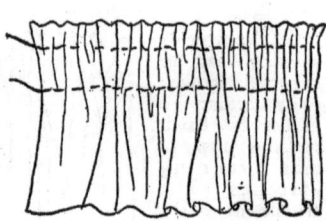

131. Double rows of shirring stay fullness

Two rows of gathers are often used in dressmaking and do not need stroking. A skirt joined to a band, a sleeve set in a cuff or sewed into the armhole, should be gathered twice so that the gathers will stay in the proper place.

The second row is made with the stitches directly in line with those of the first row and one-quarter or three-eighths of an inch below them (Illustration 131.) If there is much fullness to be gathered, the spaces between the stitches may be lengthened.

Shirring is made of successive rows of gatherings. It is used as a trimming. There are several different kinds of shirring, the use of which must be determined somewhat by the character of the material and the style of the garment. Before beginning, it is best to mark the sewing lines with a colored thread to be sure to get the rows even. This thread can be drawn out when the shirring is finished.

Gauging or French gathers—this is a style of shirring generally used where a quantity of material must be adjusted to a comparatively small space. (Illustration 132.) The stitches in this case are made unevenly: long ones on the right side and short ones on the under side of the material. Each successive row of gathers has its long and short stitches parallel, respectively, with those of the preceding row. The threads are all drawn up evenly and fastened at the ends.

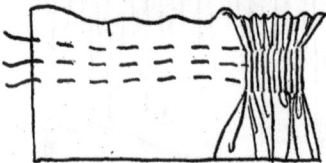

132. French gathers are very decorative

RAPID GATHERING BY HAND OR MACHINE

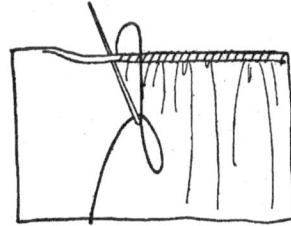

133. Whipped and gathered ruffle

To make a whipped and gathered ruffle, in fine lingerie, roll the raw edge and overhand as far as it is rolled, taking care to make the stitch below the roll, not through it. (Ill 133.) Draw up the thread as you go, making the ruffle the desired fullness. Divide the ruffle in quarters and mark them with colored thread. Make corresponding marks on the edge to which the ruffle is to be attached. Roll the edge of the garment and overhand the ruffle to it, taking a stitch in every whipped stitch of the ruffle.

Shirring can be done very successfully on the machine by using the gathering attachment. It is then necessary to mark the first line.

Successive lines may be made easily by using the gauge that comes with the machine.

Another method of shirring by any machine that has a double thread is to stitch in the ordinary way with a rather loose tension.

Use a medium-length stitch. If the pattern has no perforations to guide you, use the gauge for spacing stitchings evenly.

Pin the center of the stitchings to a table, or any flat surface. Hold all the under threads together with one hand. With the other hand, push material gently back to form shirrings. (Ill. 134.)

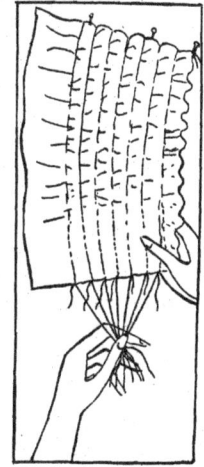

134. Machine gathering

HOW TO MAKE FUR COLLARS AND CUFFS

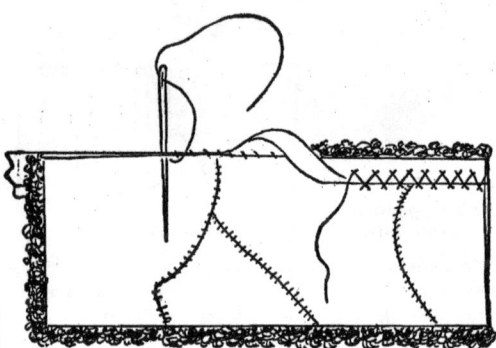

135. Finishing fur banding

For any garment in which fur is to be used, the Deltor shows how to handle it to the best advantage. However, sometimes it is necessary to mend or recut a collar or trimming band, and for such a time the following suggestions will be helpful.

Pelts should always be cut with a knife from the wrong side so as not to cut the hair.

Joinings should be made so that all the hair runs one way.

Fur should be sewed with an ordinary short needle and strong cotton thread. Number 30 cotton is about the right weight.

Lay the pelts edge to edge with the fur side down and sew the edges together with an overhand stitch (page 61). Be careful to sew through the pelts only, without catching the hair in the sewing. The hair can be pushed through to the right side with the needle and after the sewing is finished the fur can be brushed gently to make the hair lie smooth. In this way you will conceal any sign of the joining.

After the joining is made you will find on the wrong side a ridge-like seam. This seam should be dampened and the fur should be stretched out smooth on a flat board and tacked to it. The fur should be left on the board until it is thoroughly dry, which generally takes about twenty-four hours.

In the short-haired furs the hair side of the pelt can be laid next to the board, but in heavier furs the pelt is always laid face down.

FINE STITCHING FOR FINE FEATHERS

In most cases the edges of fur must be finished with braid or seam binding the color of the fur. Overhand the edge of the braid or seam binding to the edge of the fur (Illustration 135), turn it over the edge of the fur and catch-stitch it to the pelt as illustrated. Sew it on to the garment through the braid or seam binding, using a slip-stitch.

This is the best way to handle most furs. In the case of a fur in which the pelt is not the same color as the fur itself, as in undyed furs, the binding is absolutely necessary.

When the pelt is the same color as the fur, as in dyed furs or in white furs, and the hair is long enough to cover the edge of the pelt nicely, this braid or seam binding may be omitted and the sewing done right through the pelt. In this case sew the edge of the pelt to the material with a hemming stitch. This is, of course, a simpler method and it is the best method to use in sewing fur to transparent materials, for the binding or braid adds to the weight of the fur.

To sew feather trimming to a negligée, mark with sewing silk the line where the trimming is to be sewed. If there is a fine cord at the upper edge, rip it off. Arrange the upper edge of the trimming along the thread line. Sew to position, using thread of the same color to make the sewing invisible.

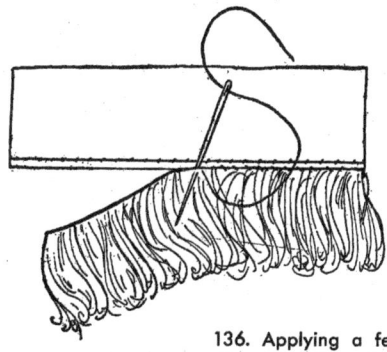

136. Applying a feather trimming to edge of a negligee

PLAITED TRIMMINGS
HOW TO MAKE THEM

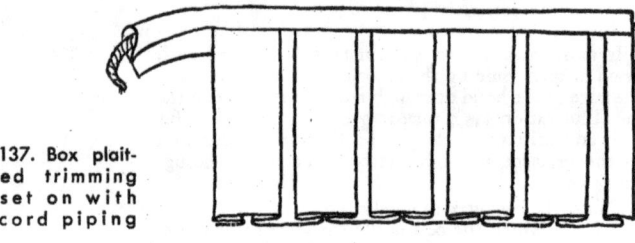

137. Box plaited trimming set on with cord piping

A box plaited trimming to be joined to a garment with a cord piping is shown in illustration 137. The strips for the plaiting may be cut bias or straight. The outer edge of the plaiting may be picoted or finished with a narrow hem.

Make the cord piping as described for a cord facing on page 75.

The cord piping and the unfinished edge of the plaiting are joined together in a plain seam. The seam is then turned down flat under the plaits and the plaits are then pressed.

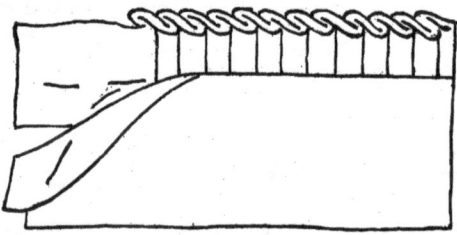

138. Side plaiting set on a straight or curved edge

A quilling or simple side-plaited trimming is shown in Illustration 138. The strips of material may be cut bias or straight and should be three times as long as the finished trimming. The outer edge of the plaiting may be picoted, hemmed or pinked, or the plaiting may be made double.

The garment edge which the plaiting is to finish should be turned under the seam width and basted. The plaiting is basted under this edge and sewed in position according to the material and finish of the garment.

TAILORING ESSENTIALS
FOR THE HOME SEWER

Many home sewers who make very successful frocks and other "dressmaker" garments are afraid to attempt a tailored garment. There is really no reason for this fear if you use a Butterick pattern and follow the directions for cutting, fitting, and putting together that are given by the Deltor.

As a matter of fact, making tailored garments for women is a much simpler operation than it used to be. There is less use of the interlinings and facings, canvas reinforcements and notched lapels than formerly; but even these details are not at all terrifying if you will keep in mind and carry out the following requisites of all tailored work.

Tailoring is really a minor operation

First of all, cut carefully. In the making of any garment cutting is important, but in nothing is it more important than in a coat or frock of heavy material. If you will follow your Deltor in laying out your pattern, and remember to use sharp shears and follow the line of the pattern exactly, you will find the basting together of the seams a simple matter.

Of course before cutting you ought to pin your pattern together as suggested on page 16, to make sure that the length is right for you; and after the garment is cut it is of the greatest importance that you mark the perforations and notches as outlined on page 34.

The next thing to remember is that any material which is going to be exposed to damp or rainy weather should be shrunk before it is cut, and this applies to everything whether outer material or interlinings. It does not, of course, apply to fur or to the silk lining, which is put in loosely, so that there is no danger of its drawing even if it does get wet.

The next thing to keep in mind is the grain of the material and the importance of folding accurately. It would be worth your while to go back to page 30 and read over again the section about the grain of a fabric.

If you have ever seen a partly made tailored garment, that is a garment made by a tailor, you have probably noticed that there is a great deal of basting about it, and this is an example you will do well to follow. It is hardly possible to do too much basting in tailoring, because it is essential to hold everything in position so that there may be no slipping or curling of edges during the stitching or after the garment is completed. The Deltor of your pattern tells you where to baste.

The tailor sets a very good example

REMEMBER, REMEMBER THESE FEW SIMPLE FACTS

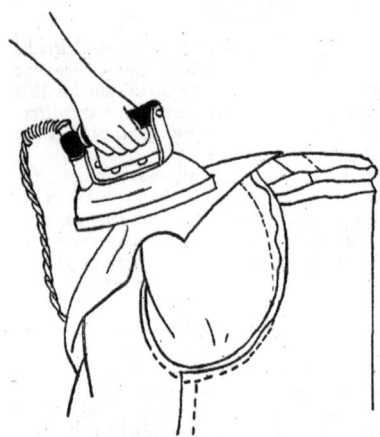

139. Smoothing out fullness in the top of a sleeve

This is a good place to pause for a short lesson on pinning and basting. Pin everything before you baste, putting in the pins at right angles with the seam. Pin the two extremities together first, and then—holding the work lightly so that bias edges will not be stretched —put in pins every three or four inches, then baste.

After you have basted and fitted a tailored garment and have done all preliminary pressing, remember that good machine stitching is essential and this does not apply only to stitching which appears on the outside. A seam which is to be pressed open must be stitched accurately, and the tension must be adjusted so that the stitch is perfect and is neither too long nor too short. When stitching heavy materials, use a fairly heavy silk or cotton and a fairly coarse needle, and be sure to watch the tension and the pressure foot.

Finally, remember to press often. A skilled tailor keeps an iron and a board at hand all the time he is working and uses them constantly, sometimes to press only a few inches, such as a shoulder seam. It may be that you will find it helpful to press your seams even before you stitch them, if the material is unusually bulky, but in any case, remember to press at each stage of the garment and not to leave it all to be done at the end.

MORE HINTS FOR THE HOME TAILORESS

Suggestions for pressing various kinds of materials are given on pages 109 to 113 in this book.

In addition to these prime essentials of all tailoring, there are a few suggestions of details that will help you in remodeling. For instance, if material is stretchy so that it sags at the edges, these may be reinforced underneath with a narrow linen tape or the selvedge of a lining material, which must, of course, be thoroughly shrunken and pressed flat before it is sewed on.

When a coat sleeve is finished without a cuff, a bias strip of interlining should be basted into the wrist just above the turning line of the hem part and the cloth turned over and catch-stitched to it. (Illustration 140.)

140. Interlining a sleeve without a cuff

There is usually more or less ease in the top of a coat sleeve. This should be distributed as best fits the figure of the person for whom the coat is being made. To shrink out the fullness at the top, slip the sleeve over the small end of a tailor's cushion. For wools, lay a damp cloth over the gathers and press carefully. (Illustration 139.) In silks, use a dry cloth and press with a warm iron.

Flat lead weights are often tacked into the bottom of a coat to weight it properly. They should be covered with the lining material so they will not wear through the lining.

Dressmaking is like playing a game. It has rules like any other game, and you must follow them to win. All rules for a coat which is to be made by a Butterick pattern are in the Deltor. Anyone who can follow simple directions, can follow these—and anyone who wants to, can make a coat.

TAILORED POCKETS FOR TAILORED JACKETS

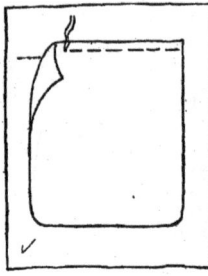

141. Applying pocket piece

In any Butterick Pattern that calls for a pocket, directions for making it are given on the Deltor, but a general acquaintance with some of the methods used by tailors is often a help in remodeling, and the following methods of making pockets may be adapted to this need by fitting the size, shape and variety to the spot where the pocket is needed.

An essential preliminary to any pocket, is to run a line of basting to mark the pocket opening, letting it show plainly on both sides of the material.

An exceedingly tailor-made appearance may be given to a boy's coat by the use of pockets with in-and-out laps.

Stitch the lap and its lining with right sides

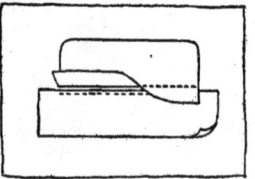

142. Setting the lap for facing

together, then turn right side out and baste. Leave the edges soft or stitch according to the finish of the garment. Press. Baste along the top, leaving the edges raw and being careful to have the lap section a trifle easy.

Baste a pocket section on the inside of the garment, placing the top half an inch above the line of basting.

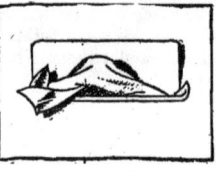

143. Pulling the facing through

Turn the garment to the outside. Cut a facing of the material about two inches wide and long enough to extend one inch beyond each end of the basting line. Lay this on the garment with its upper edge just touching the line. Baste and stitch ⅛ inch below the edge.

THE POCKET LAP HAS A VERY DIGNIFIED AIR

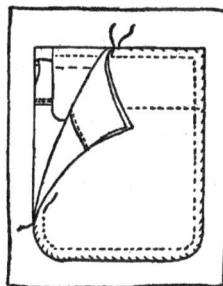

144. The way it looks from the wrong side

Lay the lap right side down on the outside of the garment, with its finished edge upward and its raw edge extending ⅛ of an inch below the line of stitching that holds the facing to the garment. Stitch the lap to the garment ⅛ of an inch above the top of the facing.

Slash between the stitchings, taking care not to cut the lap.

Press the seam of the facing open and push the facing through the opening, letting it form a binding ⅛ of an inch wide. Baste and stitch along the line where the binding joins the garment. Turn the lap down and baste close to the upper edge.

Turn the garment to the inside and stitch the facing twice near the lower edge, stitching it to the pocket section but not to the garment.

Push the lap through to the inside, with the raw edge upward, and baste to the garment just below the pocket opening.

Face the inner pocket section with a piece of the garment material about three inches wide.

Place the inner pocket section over the outer, and baste along the upper edge. Blindstitch the top of the inner section to the garment or turn it to the right side and stitch through all thicknesses just above the line where the lap joins the garment.

Turn the garment wrong side out and stitch the pocket sections together. Overcast the edges.

Finish the ends with bars on the right side.

Pull out the basting that holds the pocket-lap and pull the lap out through the opening.

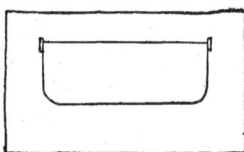

145. The finished pocket should be smooth perfection

A POCKET WITH A WELT IS EASILY MADE

This method is a good one to use when material is light in weight and you have enough to make the pocket and welt of the same material as the garment or of a contrasting material.

Run a line of basting to mark the opening of the pocket, letting the basting show plainly on both sides of the material.

Baste both pocket sections face down on the right side of the garment, with the raw edges exactly even with the line of bast-

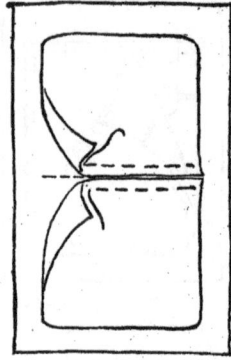

146. Applying the pieces on pocket line

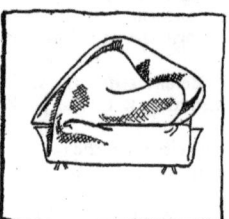

147. After stitching slit, push material thru'

148. (below) Overcast the seam edges on back

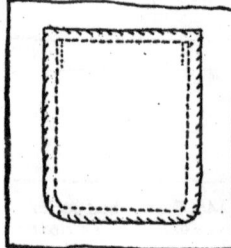

ing that marks the opening of the pocket.

Run a row of machine stitching ⅜ of an inch from each edge, leaving ¼ of an inch between stitchings, and tie the threads securely.

Slash along the basted line to within ⅜ of an inch of each end. Make a cut diagonally from that point almost, but not quite, to the stitching line at each corner, forming a ≺ at each end. Turn under the little triangle of material thus formed at each end of the pocket opening.

Push the pocket sections through the slash, creasing the lower section at indicating tailor's tacks to form a welt.

ONE PIECE OF CLOTH WILL MAKE A POCKET

149. A finished welt pocket

Press down the seam at the lower edge of the opening, and press up the seam at the upper edge of the opening. Blind stitch along the seam at the lower edge to form the welt. Sew the ends of the welt in position.
Stitch the pocket sections together and overcast edges. Press the finished pocket.

The one piece pocket

This method of making a bound pocket is good when the material is light in weight and you have enough of your garment material to make the pocket.

Run a line of basting to mark the pocket opening, letting it show plainly on both sides of the material.

Arrange the pocket on the outside of the garment with right sides together and the center over the line of basting. Baste to position. Stitch across the ends and each side of the line of basting, keeping ⅛

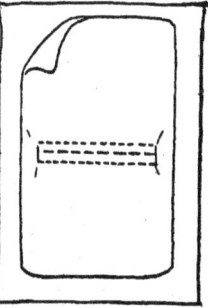

150. Applying the one piece facing

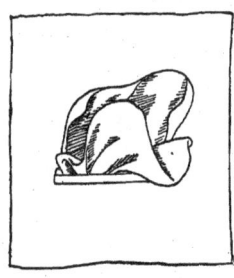

151. Pulling facing thru'

of an inch from it on each side. Slash along the basting line to within 3/16 of an inch from each end. Make a diagonal cut from that point almost, but not quite, to the stitching line at each corner, forming a ⊰ at each end. Press the seams open.

Push the pocket through to the inside, letting it

WELL MADE POCKETS ARE SMOOTH AND FLAT

form a binding ⅛ of an inch wide on the right side. This will form a tiny inverted plait at each end on the wrong side. Put crosswise stitches through the binding edges to hold them in

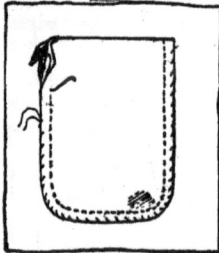

152. Keep pocket stitched while you work

shape until the garment is finished. Run lines of stitching above and below the opening, along the lines where the upper and lower bindings join the garment.

Turn to the inside of the garment and fold the upper section down. Baste and stitch the edges of the two pocket sections together, trimming off any unevenness. Overcast the edges.

153. Finish the seams with overcasting

Press the finished pocket from both the inside and outside of the garment.

154. The finished pocket

Pressing is a very important part of pocket making.

The question of whether to use a bound pocket or one with a welt depends partly upon the kind of material you are using, partly upon the place it is to be used, and partly upon your own preference. The line of a well made bound pocket is clean and inconspicuous. It seems to belong more to fine materials and a certain formality of design than to the heavy, rough type of garment. Welted pockets are often used in boys' coats and vests, and in women's street and sports clothes. In cutting a welt, be sure that it matches the part of the garment where it is to be used, both in grain of material and in design, if it is a fabric with a design.

MAKING SMART CLOTHES
MODERNIZING YOUR WARDROBE

155. These smart frocks suggest interesting possibilities for successful remodeling

Every smartly dressed woman should take stock of her wardrobe as regularly as the new season rolls around with an eye to salvaging favorite frocks for further active duty and discarding others.

It takes ingenuity to modernize one's old clothes successfully, so don't tackle the problem alone. Consult the Butterick publications, Delineator and Butterick Quarterly. In every issue you will find suggestions that can be applied to your frocks to bring them up-to-date.

As long as it is the fashion to combine two materials in one costume, remodeling is easy. The idea is this. Select a smart pattern combining two fabrics. Use

Be prepared for fashion's revolutions

KEEP YOUR FAVORITE FROCK IN STEP WITH STYLE

Successful fabric combinations

your old frock for the part that takes the most material and then buy a little new material for the rest.

Figured materials combined with plain of a harmonizing color are stunning in wool, silk or cotton. To contrast textures in matching colors is another smart trick. Combine wool with silk, crepe and velvet with chiffon, or georgette, chiffons with lace or tulle, and cottons with batiste, handkerchief linen or voile.

Thank fashion for the lace yoke and the tunic blouse

Last year's afternoon frock can be dropped low from a yoke of lace to make a stunning Sunday night frock with angel sleeves.

Skirts that seemed a total loss can now be lowered to decent length on bodice tops and combined with a new tunic blouse of lamé or satin, or you can reverse the English and make a knee length tunic of a too short frock, combining it with a new skirt. You can cut off the top of your dress altogether and substitute a new one of contrasting material.

You can make an ankle-length dance frock by cutting off last year's dipping hemline evenly below the knees and adding an 18″ band of tulle.

156. New sleeves for old frocks

A rest cure for all your tired sleeves

So often sleeves wear out before their time. Butterick has prepared special patterns to replace them, each offering a variety of interesting remodeling suggestions.

If a sleeve is worn at the elbow, cut it off here and combine it with lace or chiffon, or add a flare below the elbow (Ill. 156). If it requires a whole new sleeve, give it dolman sleeves of contrasting fabric in matching color—chiffon sleeves for a velvet frock or velvet sleeves for a crepe frock, or you can cut out worn sleeves entirely and add a contrasting bolero jacket.

DECORATIVE NECKLINES FOR FROCKS NEW OR OLD

157. A fabric bow adds a soft touch

There isn't a doubt but that in surveying your wardrobe with an eye to renovations you'll find a frock or two that can assuredly face the new season with nothing more than the addition of a fresh lingerie touch.

The Deltor comes to your assistance with many attractive suggestions for freshening your worn frocks with new collars, little cuffs, unusual bandings and those same little lingerie bows that make French frocks look so French.

The two illustrations on this page show varied versions of the smart bowknot finish that is so easily achieved with a straight strip of organdy, voile, or fabric to match your frock. The four edges may be rolled in a tiny hem or picoted. Fig. 158 shows the strip gathered at the center and inserted through bound vertical slashes; in fig. 157 it is simply tied in a knot and tacked to the neck of the frock.

You can do interesting things to dress up the neck of daughter's last year's cardigan, too. You've no idea of the swank two little buckles add to the regulation straight banding. The ends of the straight band which is stitched down and doubled to make the collar, are lined and then tacked in place after the small buckles are slipped on. (Illustration 160.)

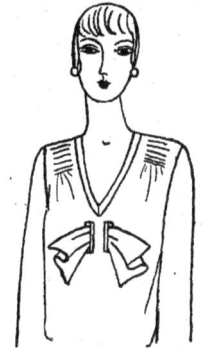

158. The more tailored bow

BLANDISHMENTS FOR A YOUNGER GENERATION

The Deltor of the Butterick Pattern shown here suggests a naive finish for a child's frock. Cut a shaped facing with ends to cross in front; stitch the

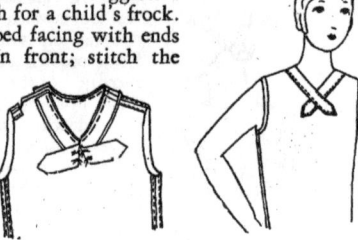

159. A crossed and stitched banding

160. For a smart young cardigan use two buckles

facing to the inside of the neck of the frock and fold it over turning in the edges; then lap the right end over the left and machine stitch to the frock all around.

Sometimes just the addition of two buttons will turn the balance of a small person's favor toward wearing last year's frock another season. The finish shown in ill. 161 is similar to that in ill. 159 except that the ends are lined and left free. Buttonholes are worked in each tab and slipped over buttons sewed to the frock.

161. Button-down tabs make her feel "grown-up"

TAILORED NECKLINES HAVE THEIR WAYS, TOO

162. Lingerie clasps of fabric for every frock

163. The tie is held in place by horizontal slashes

A straight tie with ends cut on a slant goes a long way toward giving a sports feeling to a frock to be worn with your cardigan jacket. Make the tie double and slip it through two bound horizontal slashes. (Ill. 163.)

The shaped facing is a very nice thing to know about when you are reviewing your blouse wardrobe. Stitch the right side of the facing to the inside of your blouse, turn it over and gather at the front, stitching free edges to the blouse. Tack a bowknot over the gathers. (Illustration 164.)

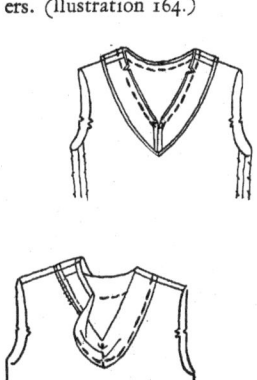

164. Three steps accomplish a smart finish

BERTHA COLLARS AND CAPELETS OFFER SUGGESTIONS

It is a smart trick to save a last year's frock for still another season by removing the sleeves and adding one of these becoming capelet or bertha collars. The Deltors in Butterick Patterns to the right and below show you how to cut and attach them to a V necked frock. The little tie at the point of the V would add a springlike touch to other frocks, too. Fig. 165 illustrates an unusual cut on which much of the smartness depends. Picot or hem it, slip it through a horizontal slash or over a collar joining and knot it softly. The butterfly bow effect in (Ill. 168) is another individual finish for the point of a bertha collar. It may be inserted through two vertical slashes or shaped in the double bow and tacked to the neck of your frock.

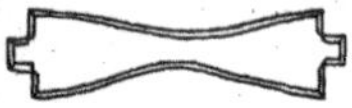

Fig. 165.

166. Tailored tie finish

Fig. 165 above shows the cut of the tie which should be knotted at the point of the V as in Fig. 167.

Fig. 167.

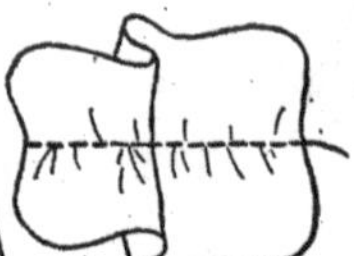

Fig. 169.

168. Butterfly bow finish

MAKING SMART CLOTHES
PROFESSIONAL PRESSING

Good pressing is a very important part of dressmaking and tailoring. Special boards and tailor's cushions may be made at home or bought from any dressmakers' supply house.

You should have either an electric iron or an ordinary iron. A six-pound smoothing-iron is a satisfactory type for pressing. *The tools are half the battle*

Next in importance to a good iron is a good ironing-board.

An ironing-board should present a smooth, firm but soft surface. It is impossible to do good pressing on a board with a surface broken by hollows or ridges, so the

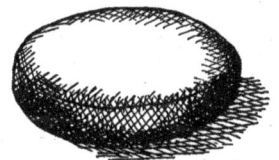

170. A tailor's cushion is not to be sat on

first essential is a smooth, hard piece of board of the desired size and shape.

The board should be covered with at least four thicknesses of cotton felt, which may be bought at any store that carries tailors' and dressmakers' supplies or with one of the heavy pads sold for the purpose. Lacking one of these, a good substitute is an old woolen blanket. Care should be taken, however, not to use pieces that have holes in them, as this might affect the evenness of the pressing surface.

A tailor's cushion is used for pressing darts and curved seams. It is ham-shaped and is stuffed tightly with cotton rags. Cut two pieces of unbleached cotton or other firm material eighteen by fourteen inches, making them narrower at one end. Round off all the edges. Stitch the seam with a close stitch.

Seams should be pressed over the tailor's cushion so that the seam edges will not be marked on the garment. In opening seams, dampen the seam if the material will permit and press slowly, bearing down heavily on the iron. Very little dampness should be used on wool materials as it flattens the texture. Little or no dampness should be used on silks. A cloth damp but well wrung may be used on these materials when necessary and their seams may be dampened slightly. *How dry can you make your pressing cloth*

A PANACEA FOR EACH OF FOUR VELVET TROUBLES

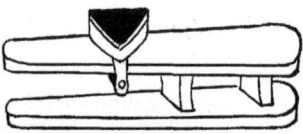

171. A Sleeve board ready for steaming or panning

A sleeve-board which can be used for sleeves and short seams can be bought either plain or fastened to a standard, or can be made from a board two or three feet long and tapering from five or six inches in width at one end to three inches at the other. The ends and edges should be rounded, and the board should be padded as described.

Pressing velvets Velvet, plush and wool pile fabrics should not be pressed in the usual way, but they can be pressed on a wire board made especially for the purpose. This board is made of fine wires set close together in a slanting position on a heavy canvas back which is tacked to a flat board. The pile sinks between the wires when pressed and is not injured. Six by eighteen inches is a good average-size board.

A seam in the edge of a facing on the front of a coat made of nap materials can be pressed by using this wire board in another way. Loosen the tacks holding the wired canvas to the board; place the part of the material that is to be pressed on one end of the wires and fold the other end of the wired canvas over the material. Place a damp piece of muslin over the canvas and press as shown in Illustration 173.

This board is rather expensive for private use, and if it is not available it is best to steam these materials in the following ways:

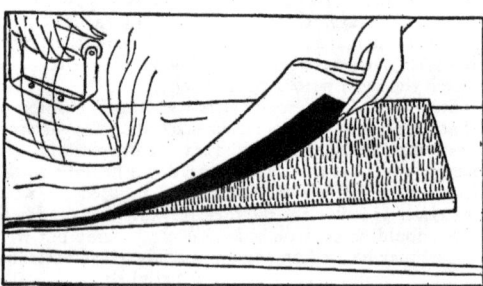

172. Using the velvet board

FURTHER TREATMENT FOR VELVET AND PILE FABRICS

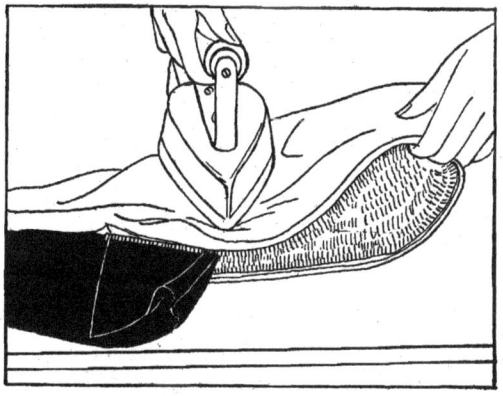

173. Double the velvet board for pressing edges

To steam a pile fabric, invert a heated iron and slip the small end of a sleeve-board through the handle. Place something under the ends of the board to hold it firmly. (Illustration 174.) Lay a damp piece of muslin over the face of the iron and draw the velvet over the muslin. The steam will have the effect of pressing velvet without hurting the pile. Seams can be opened in this way, and this method can be used on velvet, plush, velours, duvetyn and other materials with a high nap.

Almost all tailors and cleaners now have large steaming boards on which an entire garment of pile fabric can be steamed and home sewing can be made much easier by sending out work of this kind.

Velvet may be mirrored or panned by passing an

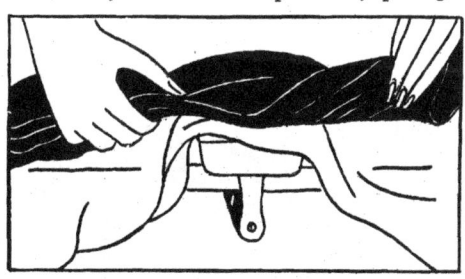

174. Steaming a pile fabric

THE EXPERT KNOWS THE VALUE OF GOOD PRESSING

iron over the surface of the velvet, ironing with the nap. After velvet has gone through this process it can be pressed as much as is necessary.

There's right and wrong in pressing

Nearly all pressing is done on the wrong side. Suitings and heavy cloth may be pressed on the right side by steaming. Wring out a cloth as dry as possible and lay it over the place to be pressed. Have the irons hot and press firmly until the cloth is nearly dry. Turn the garment to the wrong side and press thoroughly dry.

The shine which sometimes comes in pressing may be removed by placing a dry cloth over the shiny place. Then wring out as dry as possible a second cloth which has been thoroughly wet. Place it over the dry one, and with a hot iron pass lightly over the spot. If the material has a nap requiring raising, the place may be brushed with a stiff brush and the process repeated.

Many fabrics retain the imprint of the basting-thread under heavy pressing. For such material it is necessary to give a light pressing first, removing all basting-threads before the final pressing.

How to press plaits in a dress or skirt

Turn the skirt wrong side out and slip it over an ironing-board. Pin the top and bottom of the skirt to the board, taking care that the plaits lie perfectly flat underneath. In wool and cotton materials a sponge cloth may be placed over the skirt and pressed thoroughly until the cloth is dry. This method creases the material well and the plaits will stay in position for a long time.

In silk material press the plaits with an iron that is not too hot. Afterward the iron may be run under the plaits to smooth the part underneath. Slip the skirt off the board and remove the bastings.

175. For velvet seams use a wire board

SHRINKING AND STEAMING FOR "WELL MADE EFFECTS"

Surely it is not necessary to read you a lecture on the importance of knowing whether the wool material you select for your new spring suit has been duly shrunk. You know what happens to woolens that have not been shrunk the first time they get caught in the rain. They have an inconvenient way of shrinking about two and one-half inches to the yard. Nine times out of ten the lovely fabrics you see in the shops are carefully shrunk by the manufacturer before they are put on sale, but if you are addicted to bargain hunting, every once in a while you may run across a piece that has not been subjected to this treatment. If you have set your heart on having it then buy an extra two and one-half inches for every yard you need and prepare to have it shrunk. Most shops will perform this service for you, or your tailor can do it; but if by any chance you are cast away on a desert isle where you can't obtain sponging and pressing service, this is the way to go about it. **Bargain hunters should beware**

You will need a large table, an ironing-blanket and a strip of heavy unbleached muslin the width of your material and one-half its length.

Lay your material face down on the table. Wet the muslin with cold water and wring it out. Spread it out, pulling out all the wrinkles, and lay it over half of your material. Fold the other half of the material over it, roll the material and sponging-cloth together in a tight roll and let it lie overnight covered with a piece of muslin and some newspapers so that the moisture will be retained.

In the morning unroll the material, pressing it dry on the wrong side as you unroll it.

Certain wool materials, such as deep-pile fabrics, should be steamed instead of sponged. Use the same table, ironing-blanket and unbleached muslin as for sponging. Lay the material face down on the blanket; wet the muslin and lay it over the material as for sponging. Hold a moderately hot iron so that it just touches the material enough to let the steam penetrate the fabric. Pass it over the muslin, but do not let it rest on it. It must just touch the muslin. **If you can't get someone else to do it**

MAKING SMART CLOTHES
KEEP THEIR FRESHNESS

Any day may be wash day

The extensive use of fine materials has made the laundering of the modern woman's wardrobe a thing apart from the regular weekly wash. The voluminous bulky garments that formerly required back-breaking hours of washing and laborious ironing have been replaced by light scanty garments that wash as easily as a pocket handkerchief and often require no ironing at all. As far as personal garments are concerned, the wash-tub has dwindled to a wash-bowl.

When the modern woman washes her stockings, gloves, scarfs, dresses, and the dozen and one lovely etceteras that make up her wardrobe, her success depends on whether she has adjusted her washing methods to the new type of clothing.

A few labor saving rules

By following a few simple rules, the modern wardrobe can be kept immaculately clean, fresh, and attractive, with very little labor.

1. Prepare moderately warm suds, with a mild, pure soap—flakes, beads or cake.
2. Squeeze or knead the suds through the garment from three to five minutes.
3. Rinse two or three times in lukewarm water.
4. Squeeze the water from the garment.
5. Roll tightly for a few minutes in a bath towel.
6. If the colors are doubtful, remove from the towel at once and shake, preferably in front of an electric fan, until dry enough to iron.
7. Iron on the wrong side with a moderate iron before the garment has become entirely dry.

To prepare the suds: first dissolve the soap in a small quantity of hot water, then run in cooler water to bring the whole to about 100° F. This is practically the temperature of the hands, but in case of doubt use a thermometer. A moderate temperature is important. One tablespoon of soap flakes per gallon of water is a good proportion if the water is soft. Hard water requires more soap or a little borax or water softener. If the garment is so badly soiled that the suds break down, add a little more dissolved soap. Excessive suds are a nuisance, and make rinsing more difficult, but a moderate layer of suds lasting throughout the washing process indicates that the proper amount of soap has been

About suds more or less

used. With suds of this strength, thorough cleansing is easy. Scanty suds that break down during the washing indicate insufficient soap, and will give poor results.

THIS IS THE WAY WE WASH SMART CLOTHES

To wash: squeeze or knead the suds through the garment. This is a sufficiently vigorous action to remove all ordinary soil in three to five minutes. If the first suds become dark in color, it is well to repeat the washing in fresh suds. In case of muddy spots or other deeply imbedded dirt, on light-colored silk stockings, additional soap and a little light rubbing between the hands is a help. But as a rule rubbing is unnecessary and should be done lightly and sparingly if at all. It injures the fine surfaces and makes hard work of an easy task.

Washing and ironing made twice as easy

To rinse: two rinsings are sufficient if a fairly generous amount of water is used. For fast colors, water just comfortable to the hands is most pleasant. For fugitive colors, cold water retards the running of the dye. White silks are improved by an additional lightly blued rinse after they have become yellow. But if hot water, harsh soap, and direct sunlight are avoided, yellowing can be greatly retarded.

To remove the water: press or squeeze the water from the garment. Do not twist. Hard twisting strains and often breaks the fine filaments and so makes runs in stockings and other knitted garments. If ironing is not necessary, pull the garment into shape and hang it indoors away from direct sunlight and heat. Do not use clothes-pins on rayon. If ironing is necessary, spread the garment over a large bath towel or an old sheet. Cover with another towel and roll the whole together in a tight bundle. If the color is fast, the garment can remain rolled until most of the moisture has been absorbed by the towel, when it is ready to iron. But if the color is inclined to run, it is best to remove the garment from the towel immediately and shake it, preferably in front of an electric fan, or in a current of air, until it is almost dry. Press it immediately. Streaking seldom occurs in the suds; it occurs almost entirely during the drying. If the drying is hastened, as described, by removing the greater part of the water with towels and then shaking until dry enough to iron, fugitive colors can often be laundered very successfully. The old theory that a fugitive color can be set at home with salt, vinegar or other household means has proved erroneous. The only solution of this problem is to work fast. Have everything ready before starting: two bowls of lukewarm suds, two cold rinses, towels spread out, electric fan going, iron heating.

Prevent runs in stockings

Set color with salt no more

115

USEFUL POINTS ON IRONS—AND IRONING

A few matters of moisture Take plenty of time in the suds to remove the soil and loose dye, and if the first suds become badly discolored it is well to repeat the washing in the second suds before proceeding to rinse. Then work as rapidly as possible and, unless the color is a fast runner and you a slow worker, your chances of winning are good.

To iron: the degree of moisture necessary for smooth ironing depends largely on the material. Some crêpe and knitted weaves in either silk, synthetic fabrics or cotton should be ironed perfectly dry. This is particularly true of very elastic crêpe weaves that stretch badly when moist. Others require a very slight amount of moisture. The smooth flat weaves in silk, such as broadcloth and radium, require more moisture than crêpe weaves. But silks, as a rule, should be pressed when almost dry. Too much moisture, especially when combined with a hot iron, makes them stiff and paper-like. Silks should not be sprinkled. If they have become too dry, the proper amount of moisture can be restored evenly by spreading a slightly moist cheesecloth over them and rolling all together for a short time.

How hot the iron must be The iron should be only moderately hot—just a little above the temperature when it begins to sizzle. A temperature that can be used safely on cotton and linen scorches silks and destroys some types of synthetic fabrics. Fortunately there are irons on the market with a temperature control that assures the proper heat—low moderate or high—for any type of fabric. Other irons which indicate as well as control the temperature suitable for the various fabrics will soon be available.

Pressing for the most part should be on the wrong side of the material. Double thicknesses should be pressed first on the wrong side, then under a cheesecloth on the right side. The strokes of the iron should be directed with the thread of the material either lengthwise or across the material. This is usually determined by the individual weave. As a rule it is best to press first any loose dangling ends, then the sleeves, and finally the main part of the garment, proceeding usually from the top to the bottom.

Keeping plaits in their place Before laundering plaited garments, put a thread near the lower edge and at intervals of about six inches above. This holds the plaits during the washing and makes them easy to press.

WHEN FLARES ARE IN KEEP THEM IN SHAPE

We do not strongly recommend circular styles for wash materials, but some people insist upon using them. To get the best results in washing these styles, be careful to iron on the straight grain of the material, smoothing the lengthwise and crosswise threads into their natural position—never iron on the bias. Hang the garment up for two or three days and the circular parts will sag into the shape they took when the dress was first made. **The grain of goods again**

To wash a beaded or embroidered garment, use the same method as for thin crêpes. Never put a beaded garment through a wringer, for it would break the beads. Lay the garment right side down on a Turkish towel or soft pressing-pad so as not to break the beads in pressing. Embroidered garments should be pressed in this way also, as the design will be flattened if pressed on a hard surface. **When circular skirts are put into the tub**

When light-colored materials fade in the laundry and get that washed-out appearance that makes them look old, the freshness may be restored by using any of the good tints obtainable. These are dyes that do not require boiling. Some of them come in soap form and some are added to the rinsing water after the manner of bluing. They are easy to use and sometimes have quite lasting results so that it is not always necessary to use them each time the garment is washed. **Restoring that lovelyfreshcolor**

These tints come in two varieties—one that will dye any fabric, and one that will dye silk only, leaving lace trimmings untinted.

HAVE YOU ANY WOOL TO WASH THIS MODERN WAY

Washing wool is difficult

Because of the nature of the fibers of wool certain very simple precautions in washing must be observed. Each little tendril, from which woolen yarns or threads are fashioned, when examined under a powerful microscope is seen to have tiny overlapping scales which might be likened to the shingles on a house. These shingles are lightly attached as they overlap and before wool is sheared from the sheep they are lubricated at the roots with an oily substance known as lanolin, but after they are removed from their source of nourishment they show some tendency to slowly dry out. By experience as well as by laboratory experiment it has become obvious that there are certain conditions which hasten this process greatly, and with continued wrong treatment woolens shrink, become hard and yellow, and lose some of their valuable ability to keep us warm.

Four warnings in washing wool garments

There are four easily avoidable conditions which tend to destroy the softness of woolens or make them shrink or both. The first is hard rubbing while wet, the second is the placing of the material or garment in hot water, the third is a sudden change from warm to hot or cold water and the fourth is the presence of strong alkali in the water in which they are washed.

It is the rubbing together of surfaces and fibers more than any other one thing that causes woolens to shrink. Therefore, the washing should be done with the least possible agitation and friction.

Regardless of the materials to be laundered the conditions maintained should be quite the same. Even before the woolens are immersed in the water it is advisable to think about the drying, for if the day be heavy and the humidity high it is better to postpone the washing of blankets or other large pieces. However, if they must be washed on schedule regardless of the weather, you can greatly hasten the drying by turning the breeze from an electric fan over them.

It is well to measure all pieces and write down the measurements so that one need not trust to memory alone for the sizes after washing. For baby garments and woolen hosiery it helps to have shirt and hosiery frames to slip them over for quick drying.

How warm is luke warm?

The wash water must be lukewarm, but how hot is lukewarm water? If you have a thermometer it is very easy to find out just the correct temperature, for the water should be between 95° and 105° F.

SWEATERS AND STOCKINGS AND ALL MANNER OF WOOLS

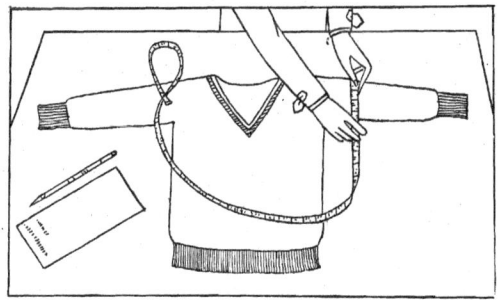

176. Measure woolen things before you wash them

This range of temperature will feel just comfortably warm to your hand, and so will not tend to draw out the natural oils within the woolen fibers. Do not forget that the temperature of each successive water in which woolens are immersed for rinsing should be the same. It is therefore advisable to draw the first of three rinse waters at the same time that the wash water is drawn. It is easiest to use flake soaps, though bar soap may be used to equally good advantage if it is made into a solution first. Draw scalding water into a bowl or tub, add soap flakes and then cold water until the water temperature has been lowered to about 100° F. A dash of borax will help to soften the water. The soap should be whisked to a suds before the garment is added and after adding, the dirt flooded out by squeezing the sudsy water through the fibers and not by rubbing.

The suds should be extremely heavy so that they will act as a cushion between the surfaces, provide lubrication, and give increased detergent power to take the place of mechanical action.

The results are equally satisfactory in hand or machine washing if the garments are not over-crowded and from ten to fifteen minutes of agitation is all that should be necessary. If garments are very much soiled it is advisable to wash in two successive soapy waters and if you are so unfortunate as to live in a region where the water is very hard it is desirable to add a very little soap solution or borax to each successive rinse.

In taking woolens from the water allow just as little pulling and stretching as possible if you would keep them in shape.

Handle with greatest care

KEEPING YOUR WOOLENS FLUFFY, SOFT AND SHAPELY

A light touch makes for the best results

Lightly squeeze out the water and if you use a mechanical wringer, the pressure of the rolls should be loosened so that the wool is not pressed hard. Put through several times instead of attempting to squeeze hard the first time, and shake to fluff.

If you are laundering small articles, squeeze by hand, taking care not to twist, place in a bath towel and then slightly twist the towel to remove water.

To dry any knit goods, lay out flat, patting into the original size and shape, being very careful to get all measurements absolutely correct and the shape just as you want it to be when dry.

Woven woolens, such as flannels, may be hung on hangers until partly dry, but they should be moved several times so that moisture has no chance to settle at the bottom. This is apt to cause a flooding of colors. It is important to press material on the wrong side with a warm iron before perfectly dry if you would regain the freshness of appearance which the garments had when new.

Blankets should either be placed on a curtain stretcher for drying or be hung on a long line. If there are colored borders they should be so hung that the stripes run perpendicular to the line and then if there is any tendency for colors to run, they will tend to run straight down instead of flooding into each other. Take the blankets from the line before they are quite dry and

Did you know that fluffy blankets are lots warmer

shake and fluff them up. They will have a better appearance and be warmer, for fluffy blankets are actually warmer than thin flat ones.

If you would keep your woolens fluffy and soft and prevent a change in size, follow these rules:

Wash before very soiled.
Choose a clear breezy day.
Measure knit goods before wetting or place on frames to dry.
Wash with aid of a mild soap containing no free alkali.
Have water temperature between 95° and 105° F.
Have wash and rinse waters same temperature.
Rinse till last water is clear.
Do not twist or ring between tight rolls.
Shape and measure knit goods.
Dry quickly, but not in strong sun.

Eleven rules to stand by

Place in draught or use electric fan for indoor drying.

REMOVE SPOTS! THEY ALMOST ALWAYS SHOW

An ink spot on Mary's new school dress, a drop of salad oil making a dark circle on a light fabric—these are household troubles which every woman faces. But what to do about it?

She tries a method of which she has heard, and it doesn't work and she believes it can't be done. But it can—the Delineator Home Institute takes out these stains every day; but always according to rule—there must be no guess-work.

Unfortunately, there is no universal stain remover. Each stain is a problem in itself and requires special treatment. Each textile fiber—cotton, linen, rayon, silk, and wool—has its own particular chemical and physical characteristics, and therefore reacts differently to the stain removers. One stain remover might be applicable to all materials, another useful in certain cases, harmful in others.

Writing ink, one of the commonest and most troublesome of stains, can be removed with almost magical ease by our new method. Then, too, this method has the added advantage of being the easiest on colored material of any treatment that will remove ink. Very often, by its use, ink can be removed from a colored garment with no damage to the dye. But this depends entirely on the dye and must be determined by first trying same treatment on a hidden part of the frock.

First obtain a small bottle of ordinary hydrogen peroxide and an ounce or two of oxalic acid crystals. Use the peroxide full strength from the bottle. Dissolve one level tablespoon of the oxalic acid crystals to a cup of water. Bear in mind that oxalic acid taken internally is a deadly poison and may easily be mistaken for water, as it is colorless and odorless. It should be labeled and kept on a high shelf in the laundry cabinet.

Put the teakettle to boil and proceed as follows. Wash or sponge the stain with soapy water. Apply a few drops of hydrogen peroxide, using a glass rod, medicine dropper, orange stick, or the stopper. If the garment is colored, use the peroxide sparingly; a drop or two at a time is enough. Hold the stain, treated with the peroxide, in the steam close to the spout of the boiling teakettle. The dark color of the ink will begin to change to yellow. Apply more hydrogen peroxide and steam again repeating until the stain has become a clear golden yellow, with every trace of the

Accidents will happen!

Ink that flows can overflow

A remedy that works

HOW TO CLEAN SPOTS WITHOUT LEAVING A RING

blue gone. Rinse in warm water and apply a drop or two of oxalic acid solution to the yellow stain now remaining in the material. If it does not disappear immediately without the aid of heat, hold it for a moment in the steam. But do not prolong the steaming here, as oxalic acid at high temperatures is destructive.

A faint blue color appearing when the oxalic acid is applied shows that the treatment with peroxide was not carried to completion. If this happens, repeat the process, and rinse thoroly thru several waters.

Success in the removal of grease spots depends to a great extent on the technique employed. There are many easy and safe dry cleaning preparations, but there is little understanding of the best method of using them. It really requires skill to remove individual spots from a garment without leaving rings, smudges or an area that contrasts with the rest of a garment by its cleanliness. But there are cases where it can be done satisfactorily, or where a slight contrast with the surrounding material is preferable to a decided spot.

Give the spot a place to go
It should be understood that while grease solvents themselves are volatile and evaporate after a certain length of time, food greases are not volatile and do not become so in being taken up by the grease remover. If not given a place to go, they are later deposited in the material on the evaporation of the solvent. They are partly absorbed and removed by a sponging cloth, but another avenue of escape should be provided in the form of a folded absorbent cloth placed beneath the spot while the sponging is going on to act as a wick in drawing solvent and dissolved grease from garment.

Be persistent, but not too generous
Another important point is a sparing use of the cleaning fluid. The sponging cloth should be barely moist, and one or two dry thicknesses of the cloth should be drawn over the moistened portion before beginning to sponge. There should be no flow of moisture from the sponging cloth to the spotted material. Very light, persistent sponging is much better than copious applications. Stroking should be carried over the spot and tapered into the fabric.

INDEX . . .

Accessories, 8
Adjustments,
   Pattern, 16, 17, 18
   Proper waistline, 18
Alterations, for figures that vary
   from the average
   after cutting,
     for large arm, 47
     for large bust, 42
     for large hips, 5, 40, 41
     for over-erect figure, 47
     for round shoulders, 46
     for sloping shoulders, 44
     for small bust, 43
     for square shoulders, 45
   before cutting,
     circular lower part, 20, 21
     dress patterns, 18, 19, 20, 21
     for large arm, 23
     for figure broad in back, 22
     for short figure, 18, 19
     for waist larger, or smaller, 49
     for tall figure, 18, 19
     sleeve patterns, 23
Basting, 33-38
   curved edges, 38
   plaits, 37
   pointed flares, 38
   seam allowance, 35
   sleeves
     in armhole, 37
   stitches,
     diagonal, 36
     even, 36
     uneven, 36
   tailoring, 95
   tailor's tacks, 34, 35
   tucks, 37
Bias bindings
   double, 71
   single, 71

Bias facings, 74
Bias-fold tape, binding with, 72
Bias strips,
   cutting, 70
   joining, 70
Bias trimmings,
   bias bindings, 71
   binding scalloped edge, 73
   cording, 75
   curved binding, 72
Bias, true, 31
Bindings, bias, 71, 72
   ribbon, 74
Black, becomingness of, 12
Blanket stitch, 87
Bound buttonholes, 78
Bound pockets, 99, 100, 101, 102
Bound seams, 60
Bound slashes, 78, 79, 105
Buttonhole stitch, 76
Buttonholes, worked, 76
   barred, 76
   bound, 78, 79
Buying your pattern,
   becoming lines, 4, 5
   correct size, 15, 16
Care of the clothes, 114-122
Catch-stitch, 61
Circular hem, 67
Cleaning,
   removing spots and stains, 121, 122
Coats,
   tailoring, 95-102
Colors,
   becomingness of, 9-13
   black, 12
   character in, 9
   color habits, 9
   cool, 9
   effect in costume, 9

Colors (*continued*)
  in texture, 12
  on figure, 12
  in eyes, 9-12
  in hair, 9-13
  for blonde, 10
  for brunette, 10
  for greying hair, 11
  for medium types, 10
  for titian, 10
  for white, 11, 12
  in fashion, 13
  in ensemble, 8
  in skin, 9-13
  pastels,
    effect on skin, 12
  response to, 9
  warm, 9
  white, 11, 12
  vitalizing effect, 10
Cutting,
  edge of pattern, 33
  fabrics, right and wrong sides, 28
  grain of material, 28, 29, 30
  lengthwise fold, 28, 29, 30
  pinning pattern, 29
  plaids, stripes, borders, 32
  preparation of fabrics, 95
  size of pattern, 15, 26, 27
  to advantage, 27
  width of fabric, 26, 27
Deltor,
  layouts, 24, 25, 26
  step by step construction, 51-57
Economy, in dressmaking, 2
Edge finishing, 71-75
Ensemble, 8
Fabrics (see also materials)
  cutting, 28, 33
  flattery in, 7
  grain of material, 28, 29, 30
  preparation, 95
  recommended for design, 14
  right or wrong sides, 28
Facings,
  applied, 74
  bias, 74
  corded, 75

neck openings, 75
neckwear, 106
ribbon,
  seam binding used as, 74
slashes, 75
shaped, 74
straight, 74
Fagot-stitch, 86
Fashion,
  in color, 13
  sudden changes of, 2
Featherstitch, 88
Feather trimmings,
  attaching, 33
Figures varying from average,
  large, 5, 6
  small, 5, 6
  becoming lines, 4, 5, 6
Fine fabrics, laundering, 114
Finishing, 50-102
  armhole, 55, 56
  buttonholes, 76, 77, 78, 79
  Deltor, step by step, 51-54
Edges, 70
  bias tape, 72
  bindings, 71, 72, 73
  curved, 72
  with bias, 70
  facings, 74, 75
  shaped, 74
  ribbon binding, 74
  feather edges, 93
  attaching, 93
  fur edges, 92, 93
  gathering, 89, 90, 91
    by machine, 91
  hems, 50, 64-69
  hemstitching, 82
    double, 84
    fagot, 84
    hand, 83, 84
    machine, 82
    picot edges, 85
    single, 84
  lingerie straps, 50, 107
  neckline, 55, 71, 105-108
  neckwear
    bandings, 106
    berthas, 108
    capelets, 108

Edges (*continued*)
  facings, 106
  tailored, 107
  plackets,
    continuous bound, 80, 81
  pressing, 109-113
  scallops, 73
    binding, 73
  seams, 59, 60
    bound, 60
    turned edges, 60
    setting in sleeves, 56
  shirring, 89, 90, 91
  stitches, 58, 61
  trimming, 94
    plaited edge, 94
  tailoring, 95
    cutting, 95
    basting, 95
    pressing, 96
    stitching, 96
Fitting, 39-49
  adjusting frock, 39
  examining fit, 39
  flat bust, 43
  large bust, 42
  large hips, 40, 41
  over erect figure, 47
  plaited frock, 49
  prominent abdomen, 48
  round shoulders, 46
  sloping shoulders, 44
  small waist, 49
  square shoulders, 45
Fold, crosswise, 30
  lengthwise, 30
French gathers, 90
French seams, 59
Fur, cutting, 92
  finishing edges, 92
  joining, 92
  pinning, 92
  stretching, 92
Gathering,
  double, single, 89, 90, 91
  French, 90
Gathers, stroking or laying, 89
Gauging or French Gathers, 90

Grain of material,
  how to determine, 29, 30
Hemming stitches
  blind, 69
  slant, 68
  slip, 69
  straight, 68
Hems
  circular skirt, 66, 67
  finishing, 50, 53
  gored skirt, 66-69
  marking, 64, 65
  stitches for, 68, 69
Hemstitching, double, single, 84
  by hand, 83, 84
  by machine, 82
  French, 85
Individuality, 2
  in dressmaking, 3
Ink stains, removing, 121, 122
Interlining,
  for coats, 97
Ironing board, 109, 110, 111
Irons, 109, 110, 111
Laundering (see washing),
    114-120
  beaded garments, 117
  circular flares, 117
  color setting, 115
  colored fabrics, 115
  embroidered garments, 117
  fine fabrics, 115
  ironing,
    circular skirts, 117
    circular flares, 117
    heat of iron, 116
    moisture of cloth, 116
    plaits, 116
  plaits, 116
  process, 114, 115
  soap, 114, 115
  water, 114, 115
  restoring color, 117
  silks, 116
  woolens, 118, 119, 120
    pressing, 112
    washing, 118, 120

Length of garment,
  how to determine the correct, 15, 64, 65
Lengthwise fold, 28, 29, 30
Let-out or Outlet seam, 35
Lines
  becomingness of, 4, 5
  berthas, 5
  hips,
    effect on costume, 5
  necklines, 4
  shoulder lines,
    effect on costume, 5
Lingerie straps, 50, 107
Machine, sewing, 62
  care, use, adjusting, 63
Materials (see fabrics),
  cutting, 28, 32, 33
  economy of buying, 7
  grain of, 28, 29, 30
  preparation, 95
  quantities to buy, 15
  recommended for design, 14
  satin, 7, 13
Markings,
  notches, 34
  pattern, 17
  perforations, 34
  tailor's tacks, 34
Nap or pile fabrics, 110
Necklines,
  bandings, 106
  berthas, 108
  bound slashes, 105
  bows, 105
  capelets, 108
  collars, 105
  decorative, 105, 108
  facings, 106
  finishing, 71
  for children, 106
  tailored, 107
Notches, 17, 34
Originality,
  in dress, 4
Overcasting, 61
Overhanding, 61
Pastels, 12
Patterns,
  adjustment, 16
  alteration, 16, 18-24

cutting, 33
edge of, 33
perforations, 17
personality in, 4
pinning, 29
markings, 17
notches, 17
selecting, 4-6
Perforations, 17, 34
Personality,
  in patterns, 4
Picot edges, 85
Plackets,
  bound, faced, 80, 81
  continuous bound, 80
  tailored, 81
Plaited trimmings, 94
Plaits,
  basting, 37
  in frock, 49
  pressing, 112
  washing, 116
Pockets,
  bound,
    with lap, 98, 99
    with flaps, 98, 99
  bound in one piece, 101, 102
  welt, 100
Pressing, 109-113
  equipment,
    cloths, 109
    irons, 109
    ironing board, 109
    moisture of cloths, 109
  pile fabrics, 110, 111
  plaits, 112, 116
  seams, 112
  sleeve-board, 110
  shrinking, 113
  sponging, 113
  steaming, 111, 113
  tailor's cushion, 109
  velvet, 110, 111
    mirroring, 110
    pressing on wire board, 110
    steaming, 111
Prints,
  becomingness of, 7, 8
  for large women, 8
  for silhouette, 8

126

Remodeling,
  combining fabrics, 104
  hemlines, 104
  necklines, 105
  sleeves, 104
Removing spots, stains, 121, 122
Satin, becomingness of, 7, 13
Seams,
  bound, 60
  finishing, 59
  French, 59
  turned-in, 59
  let-out or outlet, 35
  pinked, 59
  plain, 59, 60
  pressing, 112
  rolled, 60
  tailored, 60
  turned in edges, 60
Selecting colors, 2-13
  (see colors)
Selecting fabrics, 2-13
Selecting pattern, 2-13
Sewing-machine,
  care, use of, 62
Sleeve-board, 110
Sleeves,
  in armholes, 5
  basting, 37
  finishing armhole, 55
  setting in, 56
Skirts,
  circular, 4, 66, 67
  gored, 66
  length of, 4
  lines, 4
Slashes,
  bound, 78, 79, 105
Shirring, 89, 90, 91
Shrinking, see pressing
Smocking, 88
Sponging, see pressing
Spots and stains,
  removed, 121, 122
Steaming velvet
  and other fabrics, 110-113
Stitches,
  backstitch, 58
  basting, 34, 35, 36
  blanket, 87
  buttonhole, 76, 77, 78, 79

  catch-stitch, 61
  fagoting, 86
  feather, 88
  French tacks, 34
  half-backstitch, 58
  hemming, 66-69
  overcasting, 61
    double overcasting, 87
  overhanding, 61
  running, 58
  shirring, 89, 90
    French, 90
  slip-stitch, 69
  smocking, 88
  tailor's tacks, 34
Summer clothes,
  care of, 114, 115
Sweaters, laundering, 119
Tailoring,
  cutting, 95
  basting, 95
  interlining, 97
  preparation of fabrics, 95
  pressing, 96, 112
  pockets, 98-102
    bound with lap, 98, 99
    in one piece, 101, 102
    welt, 100
Tailor's tacks, 34
Testing
  length of pattern, 16, 17, 18,
    19. 20, 21
Trimming,
  feather edging, 93
  fur banding, 92
  plaited edge, 94
Steaming, pressing, 110-113
Velvet,
  basting, 37
  steaming, 110
  panneing, 110
Waistlines,
  adjusting in pattern, 18
  effect on figure, 6
  high, 6
  low, 6
  normal, 6
Washing clothes and materials
  (see laundering), 114-119
  beaded garments, 117

Washing clothes and materials (*continued*)
circular flares, 117
colored fabrics, 117
fine fabrics, 115
plaited garments, 116
silk hosiery, 119
silks, 116
sweaters, 119
woolens, 118, 119, 120

Welt pockets, 100, 101
Wire board, 110, 111, 112
Woolens, 118, 119, 120

Printed in the USA
CPSIA information can be obtained
at www.ICGtesting.com
LVHW042317280924
792407LV00002B/530